W9-AFO-172

HERNÁN CORTÉS

AND

LA MALINCHE

Joined by Fate:
INTERTWINED BIOGRAPHIES

HERNÁN
CORTÉS
AND
LA MALINCHE

JOHN A. TORRES

Enslow Publishing
101 W. 23rd Street
Suite 240
New York, NY 10011
USA

enslow.com

Published in 2019 by Enslow Publishing, LLC.
101 W. 23rd Street, Suite 240, New York, NY 10011

Library of Congress Cataloging-in-Publication Data

Names: Torres, John Albert, author.
Title: Hernán Cortés and La Malinche / John A. Torres.
Description: New York, NY : Enslow Publishing, 2019. | Series: Joined by
fate: intertwined biographies | Includes bibliographical references and
index. | Audience: Grade 7 to 12.
Identifiers: LCCN 2017056601| ISBN 9780766098152 (library bound) | ISBN
9780766098169 (pbk.)
Subjects: LCSH: Cortés, Hernán, 1485–1547. | Marina, approximately
1505–approximately 1530. | Mexico—History—Conquest, 1519–1540. |
Explorers—Mexico—Biography. | Explorers—Spain—Biography. |
Conquerors—Mexico—Biography. | Aztec women—Biography. |
Translators—Mexico—Biography. | Indians of Mexico—Biography.
Classification: LCC F1230.C385 T67 2018 | DDC 972/.02092 [B] —dc23
LC record available at https://lccn.loc.gov/2017056601

Printed in the United States of America

Photo Credits: Cover, p. 3 (left, bottom right) Prisma Archivo/Alamy Stock Photo; cover,
pp. 3 (top right), 47, 55, 70–71 PHAS/Universal Images Group/Getty Images; p. 8 Museo
Nacional de Arte, Mexico City, Mexico/Bridgeman Images; p. 12 Heritage Images/Hulton
Fine Art Collection/Getty Images; p. 14 Convento Agustinas, Madrigal, Avila/Bridgeman
Images; pp. 16, 27, 78–79 Universal Images Group/Getty Images; pp. 20, 60–61, 91 A. Dagli
Orti/De Agostini Picture Library; pp. 24–25 Juan Aunion/Shutterstock.com; p. 28 Luis
Castaneda Inc./The Image Bank/Getty Images; pp. 30–31 Leonid Andronov/Shutterstock.
com; p. 35 Buyenlarge/Archive Photos/Getty Images; pp. 36–37 photobeginner/Shutterstock.
com; pp. 44–45 National Geographic Creative/Bridgeman Images; p. 56 Private Collection/
Peter Newark American Pictures/Bridgeman Images; p. 58 Leemage/Universal Images
Group/Getty Images; pp. 64–65 Diego Grandi/Shutterstock.com; p. 68 Bibliotheque
Nationale, Paris, France/Bridgeman Images; p. 75 Museo Franz Mayer, Mexico City, Mexico/
De Agostini Picture Library/A. Dagli Orti/Bridgeman Images; p. 81 Stefano Bianchetti/
Corbis Historical/Getty Images; p. 85 Private Collection/Archives Charmet/Bridgeman
Images; p. 87 Private Collection/Peter Newark American Pictures/Bridgeman Images; p. 94
South African National Gallery, Cape Town, South Africa/Bridgeman Images; p. 97 Print
Collector/Hulton Archive/Getty Images; p. 102 Xavi Gomez/Cover/Getty Images; p. 103
Photo 12/Universal Images Group/Getty Images; pp. 104–105 Johan Ordonez/AFP/Getty
Images; p. 108 Chris Willson/Alamy Stock Photo.

CONTENTS

INTRODUCTION

Studying historical figures from the 1500s can be a little tricky. Take the subjects of this book—Hernán Cortés, a Spanish conquistador, and La Malinche, his interpreter and concubine who helped him topple an empire. Not many reliable documents from this time period exist, which makes it difficult to know just what happened in their lives.

Even when researchers find very old historical documents, they look at them skeptically. That's because the earliest biographies may not paint an accurate picture. They tend to retell history through one specific lens, making them biased. These biographies often exaggerated, overlooked, and fabricated reality to depict certain countries in a favorable historical light. For example, it is only during the last few decades that the legacy of explorer Christopher Columbus has come under scrutiny. He has gone from hero to mass murderer in many newer historical accounts.

And the history books haven't necessarily been accurate about the relationship between Hernán Cortés and La Malinche. Cortés is largely regarded as a womanizing, treacherous conqueror, while Malinche is often looked down upon for her relationship with Cortés. But did this enslaved Aztec woman

This nineteenth-century oil painting by Mexican artist Juan Ortega depicts Hernán Cortés, La Malinche, and Bartolomé de Las Casas.

have much of a choice? The debate over these historical figures has truly become divisive over time.

So, how should this pair be remembered? Was Cortés a conquering hero who helped spread Christianity to the Americas or a self-serving lout ready to smash anything and anyone in his path?

Was Malinche an intelligent woman who survived the only way she knew how? Did she really believe in Cortés, or was she a victim forced to do his bidding? To this day, her legacy remains perplexing.

In Mexico, Malinche continues to be a polarizing figure. Some see her as a true heroine and role model for young girls. They argue that she freed her people from the rule of a ruthless and harsh empire. But others see her as a traitor to her people, a woman who helped destroy the indigenous culture and empire that ruled the land for generations. In fact, in Mexico today to call a person a *Malinchista* is an insult meaning to betray one's culture.[1]

Right or wrong, good or bad, the indisputable truth is that Hernán Cortés and Malinche came together through a series of random events and wound up re-shaping the course of Mexico, Spain, and, in part, Central and South America.

Others have taken it farther. Mexican historian and writer Octavio Paz wrote in 1950 that the actions of Cortés and Malinche sparked a national identity crisis for Mexico and its inhabitants. The crisis, Paz wrote, affected the confidence and spirit of the Mexican people for centuries. This is a theory that many still support today.[2]

But does it have any merit? This book uses a combination of historical documents, essays, and modern-day perspectives to give you a better idea of who Cortés and Malinche were. Understanding this controversial pair, however, requires a grasp of the brutal age of exploration and colonization that marked the fifteenth and sixteenth centuries. That's where we'll start.

SPANISH CONQUERORS

Conquering and colonization quickly defined a period well known for exploration. But it all began as a race for spices by European countries such as Spain, Portugal, France, and England. While spices may seem like a strange thing to pursue, they were hard to come by during the 1500s. Refrigerators did not exist during this era, and spices from Asia could preserve meats and fish, stopping them from going bad.

The Europeans had just one problem: there was no easy way to get the spices. The Silk Road, the main route Europeans took to Asia, tended to be impassable because of ongoing military conflicts in the region. Reaching Asia by land also proved costly, as making the trip required not only manpower but gold to pay for the spices as well. Transporting valuables made the traders vulnerable to attack.

So, European rulers sent out ships with soldiers, navigators, and explorers. They would procure the spices by sea rather than by land. Only, while trying to reach Asia, European explorers happened upon the Americas instead. In the so-called New World (not new, of course, to the indigenous peoples living there), the explorers set up colonies.

Columbus Finds a Way

When Christopher Columbus first landed on the island he named Hispaniola—home to the Dominican Republic and Haiti—he had been searching for a way to Japan, China, and India. Born in Genoa, Italy, Columbus believed he could find Asia by sailing west. He believed, rightfully so, that the world was round. From there, he traveled to Portugal, where he lobbied the monarch to fund his idea and provide him with ships and a crew. At that time, Portugal led the world in exploration. In fact, one of its monarchs, Prince Henry the Navigator, even started a school for would-be explorers. He sent them to Africa's west coast.

But Portugal rejected Columbus as well, prompting him to go to Spain. King Ferdinand and Queen Isabella agreed to fund his mission, and after three months of sailing across the Atlantic Ocean, Columbus landed on an island in the Caribbean now known as Hispaniola. The year was 1492. While Columbus's legacy has come under fire in recent years—with cities such as Los Angeles, California, and Seattle, Washington, no longer celebrating the national holiday in his honor—some people still hail the explorer as a hero. They praise him for spreading Christianity from Europe to the Americas. Because he was Italian, many people of Italian descent applaud Columbus's efforts. Italian American Heritage Month falls in the month of October, the same month that the federal holiday in his honor occurs.

Columbus sailed overseas during a time when European rulers found the prospect of claiming undeveloped lands as exciting as pinpointing new and safer routes to trade and collect spices. Expeditions also gave the monarchy favor with the powerful Catholic Church, since explorers could spread Christianity all over the world.

Artist Sebastiano del Piombo painted this portrait of Christopher Columbus in 1519. It is featured at the Metropolitan Museum of Art in New York.

Spices Alter History

Five hundred years ago, spices such as pepper, cinnamon, clove, and nutmeg were as valuable as gold. These spices were in such high demand that European countries sent fleets of ships across unchartered seas in search of new ways to reach the Far East. Spice traders and their armies in the Middle East and Africa typically guarded the land routes.[1]

The search for spices spurred a wave of colonialism that created vast empires. People used these spices both to preserve food and flavor it. In addition, the rich used spices to create perfumes and embalm the dead. The spices also helped bitter medicines taste better.

To put the value of spices into perspective, consider that the English and the Dutch waged war on each other in Indonesia because of the vast number of nutmeg trees there. In the 1600s, a tiny Indonesian island named Run became important to the two countries because of its glut of the trees. England eventually turned over Run to the Netherlands in exchange for an American island—Manhattan in New York! [2]

Famous Portuguese explorer Vasco de Gama listed Christianity and spices as his two main reasons for exploring and finding new routes to India and the East. The largely Christian European nations also wanted to stop the spread of Islam. A few hundred years had passed since the Crusades. During these wars between Christians and

Nutmeg trees were once more valuable than gold and a source of conflict between countries.

This fifteenth-century oil painting of Spain's Catholic monarchs Ferdinand II of Aragon and Isabella I of Castile hangs in a Spanish convent.

Muslims, which took place primarily between 1096-1291, the two religious groups fought for control over sites they both considered sacred. Even after centuries passed, tension lingered between Christians and Muslims[3] because of the Crusades. So, Christian missionaries and religious clergy longed to convert as many people as possible to their faith. They accompanied explorers to establish churches and convert indigenous peoples to Christianity. They considered it a mission from God to spread the gospel to those who had never heard it. But, of course, indigenous peoples had their own belief systems, religious organizations, and gods.

In addition to clergy, armies traveled to the Americas to claim and guard the lands explorers reached. European monarchs hoped to use exploration as a means to profit. The Americas represented not only a chance to expand a country's glory and to spread Christianity but also a new source of income, as gold could be found there.[4]

Spain, with its confidence in an Italian named Columbus, suddenly rose to the position of a world power by claiming the entire North American continent as its own. Columbus made several more journeys to the Americas, reaching Jamaica, Venezuela, Costa Rica, Nicaragua, Honduras, and more. After Columbus, the line of explorers and conquerors Spain sponsored grew rapidly. These men included Alonso de Ojeda, Vicente Pinzón, Juan Díaz de Solís, Vasco Núñez de Balboa, and Ferdinand Magellan.

The goal of exploration was not always riches, spices, or religion. In one case, immortality inspired a voyage. Spanish explorer Juan Ponce de León set sail to find the mythical fountain of youth. According to legend, water from the spring restored the youth of those who drank or bathed in it. Ponce de León did not find a spring with youth-giving powers, but he did reach Florida. The first Spanish establishment in North America soon followed with an encampment in the Florida city of St. Augustine.

Disease: The Deadliest Weapon

Exploring and then establishing new colonies wasn't possible without conquest, since people already lived on the lands the explorers sought to claim as their own. The Spaniards excelled at conquering, as the battles they waged against the indigenous populations they encountered were gross mismatches. The conquistadors had the advantage of armor, weapons,

Spanish explorer and soldier Juan Ponce de León sailed with Columbus on his second voyage to the Americas. Ponce de León explored Florida.

gunpowder, horses, and cannons, all of which made it easy for them to defeat their Native American foes. They were also armed with a more deadly weapon and used it unwittingly without abandon—disease. Indigenous peoples had never been exposed to European diseases such as smallpox, chicken pox, measles, or influenza, so more often than not, their immune systems could not fight them off. If a Spanish settler were sick, the disease would spread among the native population like wildfire, killing thousands.[5]

The Columbus expedition was a case in point. He wrote in his journals about how friendly and accommodating the Taíno people were when he first landed on San Salvador. They brought him gifts of cloth and parrots and put down their weapons. Columbus went on to establish a settlement and city on nearby Hispaniola. Fewer than fifty years later, European diseases had decimated the indigenous population. Estimates of the Taíno population of Hispaniola vary wildly, with a number of sources reporting that hundreds of thousands of Taíno lived on Hispaniola upon Columbus's arrival. By 1548, however, fewer than five hundred Taíno lived on the island. Smallpox, influenza, cholera, typhus, and other viruses had killed them.[6] In fact, a smallpox-infected slave brought to the Americas may have inadvertently helped Cortés overwhelm the Aztecs and conquer Mexico.[7]

The Europeans and Native Americans also swapped diseases. Although the Europeans undoubtedly spread more illness, including the bubonic plague, researchers hypothesize that the indigenous peoples with whom Columbus and his crew had intimate relations likely exposed them to syphilis, a debilitating sexually transmitted disease. Once the crew returned to Europe, syphilis spread throughout the continent and even into North Africa.[8]

Disease in the New World

Perhaps you've heard of the "black death" that decimated Europe. Historians estimate that the bubonic plague killed more than twenty million Europeans between 1347 and 1352. While history books have devoted a great deal of attention to the plague, they haven't focused nearly as much on the wave of infectious diseases the Spanish conquistadors brought to the Americas. These illnesses proved deadly to the indigenous population, who had no natural immunities built up to combat them.

On the island of Hispaniola alone, 95 percent of the population died after contracting illnesses that Columbus and his crew introduced.[9] These diseases included diphtheria, yellow fever, scarlet fever, and whooping cough. The Europeans could not understand why scores of Native Americans were dying. They did not understand that the indigenous population had never been exposed to such illnesses.

As Stephen Prescott, president of Oklahoma Medical Research Foundation, put it, the arrival of the Spanish "launched a clash of infectious diseases."[10] Ultimately, up to eighteen million indigenous peoples died after Columbus's arrival. This estimate does not include the casualties suffered in other parts of the Americas.[11]

The intermingling of ethnic groups did not solely have negative consequences. For instance, the Europeans and indigenous peoples exchanged ideas and customs about how to harness natural resources and forge metal. They also exchanged foods. The colonists planted sugar and coffee from Europe, finding that they grew well in the Americas. In turn, the native peoples introduced the Europeans to maize, cassava, potatoes, sweet potatoes, and tomatoes.

European exploration and settlement of the Americas can still be felt today. There, the colonists found quinine, a cure for malaria, the deadly mosquito-carrying disease. Found in the bark of cinchona trees, quinine is a bitter-tasting substance that the indigenous peoples knew well. The Taíno and other Native Americans were expert herbalists.

The legacy of the conquistadors would have turned out very differently if it had ended with a quest for spices and medical remedies. But it didn't. The Europeans knew that settling their new colonies required a great deal of work. They needed laborers to build homes, tend to animals, and work farms and plantations. Rather than pay people for this labor, the Spaniards, Portuguese, and other Europeans sought free labor in the form of slaves. They raided the West African coast, chaining and enslaving the inhabitants.[12] The transcontinental slave trade extended into the United States, where it thrived until the 1860s.

Even after slavery ended, African Americans faced racially motivated violence and fierce discrimination that made it difficult for them to move up in society. They worked largely as tenant farmers and domestics for white employers. Without equal rights and few job and educational prospects, they continued to live an existence not much different from slavery. Throughout the Americas today, people of African descent still fight for recognition and equal rights. The descendants of slaves say they face enormous racial bias that results in housing, employment, and other forms of discrimination. Meanwhile, indigenous peoples in the Americas are marginalized as well. Efforts have grown to preserve their dialects, religions, and customs. As a result of intermarriage, however, large numbers of Latin Americans share both indigenous and European ancestry. And many have African ancestry, too.

Painter Peter Johann Nepomuk's portrait of Hernán Cortés shows the Spanish explorer in full battle armor. The painting is displayed in Italy.

The Spanish age of exploration shaped the world we live in today both positively and negatively. For Europeans, the exploration resulted in the acquisition of land and natural resources. For West Africans, the Taíno, Aztecs, and other indigenous peoples, the results of exploration were catastrophic. They not only lost their freedom, land, and customs, but many also paid the ultimate price—their lives.

By the time Hernán Cortés reached Mexico, the Spanish exploration and exploitation machine was thriving.

HUMBLE BEGINNINGS

Like so many influential people throughout history, Hernán Cortés did not always seem destined to leave his mark on the world. He was born in 1486 to Martín Cortés de Monroy and Catalina Pizarro Altamirano in the town of Medellín, Spain.

Growing Up in Medellín

The ancient village sits in the north-central section of Spain and remains tiny to this day, with a population of fewer than three thousand residents. It is named for the Roman military general Quintus Caecilius Metellus Pius and was nothing more than a military base when founded. Mainly, the general used it as a center of operations for his military campaigns during the Sertorian War. In Latin, the town was known as Metellinum. It eventually became known solely as Medellín. Although Medellín is small, other cities in Spanish-speaking countries bear the name in its honor. This includes Medellín, Colombia, the most famous of such cities.

Cortés is by far the best-known person to call Medellín home. His parents came from a long line of nobility, and their names carried great weight and honor. But their distinguished background did not translate into great wealth. On the contrary, they often struggled to support their family.[1]

In the fifteenth century, Medellín resembled other Spanish towns and cities in that it contained three different cultures: Christian, Muslim, and Jewish. While Cortés wrote many letters throughout his life, often documenting his accomplishments and challenges, he rarely mentioned Medellín or his childhood.

The numerous paintings, sculptures, and statues that honor Cortés normally depict him in battle gear as a warrior conquering new lands for the Spanish Crown. But he wasn't so mighty during childhood. Rather, Hernán was a frail and sickly infant who suffered from several childhood maladies, including colic. Some attribute his sickly state to the fact that his mother chose to have a wet nurse breast-feed him instead of doing so herself. His mother feared the effects nursing might have on her body, so she avoided feeding him in this way at all.[2]

The man who would bring down the Aztec Empire and conquer Mexico was frail and sickly as a child.

Eventually, Hernán grew stronger and healthier, although he appeared to be prone to illness his entire life. As a child, he loved playing outdoors, pretending to be mixed up in one adventure or another. He and his friends would pass the time playing and romping around a small abandoned castle in the town that the Spanish used in the wars against the Moors, a North African ethnic group. Some say that the experience of playing in a castle and pretending to attack it with his army of friends actually helped prepare Hernán for his later military conquests and escapades.[3]

This photograph of an old castle and bridge in Medellín, Spain, shows Cortés's native landscape. He and his friends liked to play in abandoned castles.

Early accounts of his youth describe Hernán as clever, smart, and very argumentative. From an early age, he admired the accomplishments of his idol, explorer Christopher Columbus. The family did not have much money to send Hernán away to school, but they scrimped and saved to pull enough together by the time he turned fourteen.

A Squandered Opportunity

The family sent him to Salamanca to live with his father's sister Inez de Paz and attend the nearby university to study law and grammar. Incredibly, the University of Salamanca still exists today. Founded in 1134, it is Spain's oldest university and the world's third oldest to run continuously. Hernán's parents hoped that legal training there would help him elevate the family to a more comfortable lifestyle. Away at university, Hernán excelled

The Moors

Medieval Europeans used the term "Moors" to describe all Arabs, European Muslims, and North African Berbers. But the term more accurately refers to the Muslims of the Middle Ages who occupied the Maghreb region of northern Africa and the Iberian Peninsula. These individuals waged war against the Roman Empire and, later, the Christian kingdoms of Europe.[4]

In the year 711 CE, Moorish troops from North Africa led the conquest of the Iberian Peninsula, which included Spain and Portugal. Later, the Moors expanded into Sicily.

Significant cultural, language, and religious differences separated the Moors from those they conquered. This created conflict that led to centuries-long wars. The Spanish called the wars Reconquista, which means "Reconquest."

The conflicts that arose were not new. Roman historian Cornelius Tacitus described how the Moors revolted against the Roman Empire in 24 CE. Unable to topple the Romans, the Moors inhabited North Africa for generations before invading Europe.

Muslim rule ended in the late 1400s after the Granada War in Spain. But the Moorish influence lives on through food, architecture, language, religion, and literature.

This painting shows King Afonso IV of Portugal and King Alfonso XI of Castile battling Sultan Abu al-Hasan and Yusuf I during the Crusades.

This statue of Hernán Cortés in Medellin, Spain, portrays him as the man who conquered Mexico and spread Christianity there.

in just about every facet of life—outside the classroom, that is. He learned to shoot, ride horses, fence, and use swords. While such skills would benefit him as a conquistador, they did not put him on the path to practice law. In the end, Hernán did not fare well enough in the classroom to remain at the University of Salamanca. He ultimately returned to Medellín without his degree.

According to some reports, Hernán fell ill. Others say he ran out of money. In any case, Hernán was not yet sixteen and, much to his family's disappointment, a college dropout.[5] Like many teens and young people who get a taste of independence, Hernán found it very difficult to get along with his father after returning home. He disliked the strict rules his family imposed on him, so he often fought with them.

He also clashed with townspeople, as his opinionated and stubborn nature tended to get him into trouble. His many fights sometimes attracted the attention of the authorities. And the fact that Hernán bedded many of the women in town did not help his reputation. His sexual relationships alarmed his pious parents, who worried about Hernán's eternal salvation.

Finally, Hernán's father decided to find an employment opportunity for him to get him out of Medellín. A job opportunity would not only give Hernán worldly experience but also help him provide for his family. Around this time, King Ferdinando I of Spain ordered more expeditions to the New World, primarily to the Caribbean, to continue Columbus's efforts there from years earlier.

Hernán was to travel with a very influential Spaniard named Nicolás de Ovando, a close friend of his father. Just before they set sail, a jealous husband found Hernán in a compromising position with his wife and nearly killed him. During the attack, Hernán fell off the roof and broke his leg. His leg healed slowly and left him bedridden with a dangerously high fever for weeks.

This is an aerial view of Old Town Valencia, Spain. As a young man, Cortés admired the city's thriving culture. He spent a couple of years there finding himself. His family may have thought his time in the city was a waste of time, but in Valencia Cortés set goals for his life after leading a rather aimless existence. His soul searching in the town likely contributed to his decision to become a conquistador and his thirst for power and riches.

The ships sailed without him. Hernán's amorous misadventure had cost him dearly.[6]

Humbled and bruised, Hernán stayed with his parents during his recovery and left as soon as he could. He spent the next year traveling around Spain but ultimately decided against the vagabond life. Eager for adventure and to make a name for himself, Hernán journeyed to Italy, where Spain was fighting a war against the French. He learned that he could rise to prominence and improve his station in life by doing well in battle there.

Hispaniola Governor Nicolás de Ovando

In 1460, Nicolás de Ovando was born into a wealthy and noble family from Madrid. He became a soldier and a knight of the Order of Alcántara, similar to the famed Templar Knights. Because of his family's many connections, Ovando landed one of the most important positions in the expanding Spanish Empire: governor of Hispaniola and the Indies. Christopher Columbus personally recommended him for the role.

Unfortunately for the indigenous inhabitants of the region, particularly the Taíno Indians, Ovando's noble ways did not extend to them. He proved to be a brutal and unforgiving ruler. He ended rebellions with massacres and eliminated any of the native peoples who opposed him. He forced the indigenous population into slavery, and many died mining for gold to send back to Spain. He also took their crops to feed the growing number of Spaniards settling in the Americas.

Eventually, Ovando returned to Spain, where he lost his title as governor because of his vicious treatment of Hispaniola's people.

But the teen was easily distracted and while making his way to the battlefront, he encountered pretty girls and gambling in the town of Valencia, on Spain's southeastern coast. He never made it to Italy and stayed in Valencia until he had squandered what little money he had.[7]

Heavily influenced by nearby Italy, Valencia had a number of fine silks and tapestries Hernán had never seen before. What's more, the women stood out as the "most beautiful, luxurious, and agreeable that one can imagine."[8] It's no wonder the young man stayed there for as long as he could, about two years. But he didn't waste these years simply chasing women and gambling. In Valencia, Hernán decided who and what he wanted to be. Tired of a humdrum life in Medellín, Hernán saw what the world could offer someone with ambition.

He no longer wanted to simply be rich. He wanted opulence. He wanted to live the life of a king. He wanted to have titles and money and power. He wanted to win people's admiration.[9]

So, Hernán returned to his parents in Medellín, determined to get on a ship and accomplish his dreams in the Americas. He wanted to find Ovando, named governor of Hispaniola and the Indies, and make amends.

This time, he would not be so careless with his future.

THE NEW WORLD

With a new outlook on life, Cortés resolved his family conflicts and behaved more maturely. His parents decided to help him find a way to the Americas. They saved money for a voyage and eventually Cortés found a trader planning to take five ships loaded with goods overseas. The year was 1506, and nineteen-year-old Cortés booked passage on one of the ships. He had two goals in mind: to find Ovando and to get rich.[1]

Starting Over

He landed in Santo Domingo, now the Dominican Republic's capital. There, he received a house and land for farming. He was told that one day he would rise to a position of great authority. But Cortés reportedly wanted an important military position right away. He scoffed at the idea of being a farmer and that his first task entailed sending reports to Spain about the island's vegetation and agriculture.

For about the next five years, Cortés exaggerated the extent of his schooling, particularly his legal training. Through his deceit he became a notary in the Dominican province of Azua, even though he lacked the qualifications. Notaries oversee the signing of important legal documents. The position, however,

Hispaniola

The island of Hispaniola is the second largest in the Caribbean. It houses two countries: the Spanish-speaking Dominican Republic and the Creole-speaking Haiti. In 1492, Columbus arrived there and established a Spanish colony. It stands out as the first permanent European settlement in the Americas, but the European invaders nearly wiped out the Taíno people who lived on the island.

Hispaniola is the twenty-second largest island in the world and served as a base of operations for explorers, including Cortés, who would later settle in places such as Cuba, Mexico, and parts of Central and South America. The island contains mountain ranges, plains, and beautiful coastlines. Its main exports include coffee and tobacco.

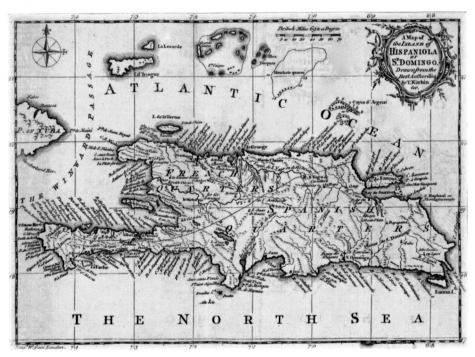

In 1758, Thomas Kitchen created this map of Hispaniola, which Christopher Columbus famously explored and Spain colonized.

Today, the Dominican Republic's beaches are a popular tourist destination. In contrast, Haiti is one of the poorest nations in the Western Hemisphere. Home of Toussaint Louverture's famous slave rebellion in 1791, Haiti's mostly black population faced discrimination from other countries afterward. Powerful nations refused to trade with Haiti. This history and, more recently, corrupt dictators and natural disasters, have ravaged the country.

Spain influenced the architecture of Santo Domingo, the Dominican Republic's capital. The island of Hispaniola houses both the Dominican Republic and Haiti. While the former is a tourist attraction, the latter has struggled to overcome poverty and natural disasters.

dissatisfied him. It was a far cry from his dreams of glory. So, Cortés spent much of his free time gambling and womanizing. Rumors spread that he'd contracted syphilis as a result of his misdeeds.[2] If so, he was able to bounce back from this very serious sexually transmitted disease. (Although syphilis still exists today, the invention of penicillin in 1928 has made the disease easier to treat than in Cortés's day, when it often proved deadly.)

Fate finally interrupted the easygoing lifestyle that bored Cortés in Hispaniola. The Spanish Crown decided to expand its empire by sending an army and ships to invade and conquer nearby Cuba. One of Ovando's top men, Diego Velázquez, had the task of leading the expedition. During the trip, Cortés was named treasurer's clerk, an important and prestigious position. It required him to collect taxes for the monarchy and send the gold back to Spain.

In Cuba, life improved drastically for Cortés. By the time he turned twenty-six, he became Velázquez's personal secretary. He also received a large swath of land from which he mined an enormous amount of gold, making him very wealthy. He fathered a little girl with one of the indigenous women and established a large hacienda. Hernán Cortés was finally an important man.

But the peace and good times would not last, as Cortés and Velázquez had several disagreements. Eventually, Velázquez had Cortés arrested for trying to complain about him to Spain's king and queen. Later, when Cortés broke his promise to marry a noblewoman named Catalina Juárez, Velázquez arrested him again and put him in stocks—wooden boards used to punish, restrain, and humiliate so-called offenders. (In the twenty-first century, stocks are occasionally still used but have widely been condemned as cruel and unusual punishment.)

Cortés eventually escaped, but he and Velázquez remained estranged for years. The men finally reconciled when Cortés agreed to the marriage. Many years later, however, he would be accused of murdering Catalina Juárez.

No longer secretary, Cortés had to move to another part of Cuba. Velázquez soon called him back into service, however, asking Cortés to lead an expedition with six ships and three hundred men to find his missing nephew. But the nephew returned before the voyage started, and Velázquez cancelled the expedition.

In a defiant move, Cortés decided to take the ships and the men anyway. He set sail on November 18, 1518, on a mission to explore and establish trading routes. But first he made several stops in other Cuban ports and collected more ships, find financial backers, and enlist soldiers. When the fleet finally left Cuban waters, Cortés had eleven ships and more than six hundred men.[3]

Cortés, having experienced life in the Caribbean, ordered special armor made from cotton that could stop the very light arrows fired by the native people of these lands. The unique armor would not only save money but also space on his ships.

Life in Mexico

He landed on Cozumel on the Yucatán Peninsula, now Mexico, and his life changed forever. Cortés ordered his men to treat any natives they crossed with kindness and respect. But he learned that the captain of the first ship to land had mistreated the indigenous people, mostly the Maya, taking some prisoner and plundering their town.

Cortés landed in Cozumel, Mexico. Centuries later the island would become a popular tourist destination owing to its beaches and nightlife.

This infuriated Cortés, who ordered the captain's arrest. The crew argued that most of the natives had fled into the interior of the country. They said they hadn't plundered the town but merely helped themselves to what the Maya left behind. This explanation did little to calm Cortés since the Maya had left behind food, slaves, and women, many of whom the crew abused. Cortés freed the imprisoned natives and gave them all gifts.[4]

He put the captain in a cell for a short time. This impressed the Maya and made them respect the Spaniard. They viewed him as a trustworthy, noble, and enchanting man. Cortés was a powerful speaker and made use of his talents to spread the gospel of Christianity.

The natives allowed him and his priest to perform a Catholic mass, during which he gave the homily, or sermon. He told the indigenous people that their idols were evil and questioned why they worshipped many gods, when there was really just one—Jesus Christ. He convinced them to crush their idols and statues and convert to Christianity. He promised that the harvest and the crops would be better than ever if they listened to him.[5]

Cortés had his carpenters construct a Catholic altar and even fashion a huge wooden cross. According to his letters, the Maya revered and respected the cross. This accomplishment made him proud because the Maya had had their own religious traditions—made up of various deities, purification rituals, priests, and so forth— for millennia.

Cortés's seeming kindness to the Maya shows what a shrewd man he was. He had won their trust and quickly established a settlement named Villa Rica de la Vera Cruz. The name translates to "Rich Town of the True Cross." It references the amount of gold and riches in the area and the fact that Cortés arrived there on the Christian holiday Good Friday, which commemorates Jesus's crucifixion.

Cortés sent back taxes to the Spanish Empire and made it known that the indigenous people were converting to Christianity. This pleased both the monarchy and the church and also prevented Cortés from getting into trouble for having disobeyed Velázquez and absconding with ships, provisions, and men.

During his stay on Cozumel, Cortés met a Spanish conquistador named Gerónimo de Aguilar. The settler had spent eight years as a prisoner of the Maya in Mexico. Meeting

Gerónimo de Aguilar

Gerónimo de Aguilar belonged to the Catholic religious order known as the Franciscans. He set out to spread Christianity in the Americas without the faintest idea of the significant role he would play in Spain's conquest of Mexico.

And it was all due to a shipwreck.

Aguilar had established a mission and settlement in Panama. After disputes with other officials, he headed to Hispaniola. He traveled with a ship, small crew, legal documents, and gold. But en route to Hispaniola, the ship ran aground and was shipwrecked just off the Yucatán Peninsula. There, the Maya captured Aguilar and a dozen survivors. They sacrificed a few to their gods and enslaved others.

Aguilar, afraid he would be sacrificed, too, escaped with one of the sailors. They found their way to a neighboring group of Maya, who kept them captive but treated them much better than the first tribe. During his eight years in captivity, he learned to speak a Mayan dialect. His fluency in the indigenous language would change the course of history after he met Cortés.

Aguilar helped Cortés immensely, for he had learned a Mayan dialect and could translate.[6]

Aguilar's presence would help pave the way for one of history's most influential partnerships. Soon after he and Cortés met, La Malinche entered the picture. The fateful encounter took place after Cortés' expedition sailed westward, stopping in an area known as Potonchán. A hostile tribe of Chantal Maya people met Cortés and his men. The Spaniards, with superior weaponry and armor, defeated the tribe and took many of the warriors prisoner. He later integrated them into his army.[7]

More battles followed over the course of the next few weeks until Cortés and the conquistadors decimated the indigenous tribes in the region. As part of the peace offering, the surviving natives offered Cortés and his men gifts, including slaves. They provided twenty women, lizards, and dogs as part of their peace offering. The women included La Malinche, then known as Malinalli.

Cortés initially awarded Malinalli to his captain, Alonzo Hernández Puertocarrero. But he took her for himself when he learned that the young woman could speak both Maya and Nahuatl. The peoples of southern Mexico, including the Aztecs, spoke Nahuatl.

Three weeks passed, and Cortés and his crew—complete with their new "gifts"—set sail once again.

LA MALINCHE

Just who was La Malinche? Before learning about her relationship with Hernán Cortés, it's necessary to answer that question. When she met the conquistador, she was an enslaved teen named Malinalli, but it's important to note that she was not born into bondage.

A Mother's Betrayal

According to most accounts, she was born in 1502 and named after a kind of wild grass. Because of her name, historians believe that she was probably born on May 12, 1502, since the Aztec calendar assigns the name Malinalli to a specific birth date. If historians are correct, she was just sixteen when she first met Cortés.[1] The conquistador, on the other hand, would have been about twice her age.

Malinalli came from an Aztec family in Coatzacoalcos, a pre-Columbian Mexican province by the Gulf Coast. The daughter of an Aztec chief, she belonged to a privileged class of indigenous peoples. Her tribesmen likely referred to her with more respectful name Malintzin. But in many ways, her life probably resembled that of other young native women.

This illustration shows a bustling marketplace in Tenochtitlan, the Aztec Empire's capital. As soon as Cortés entered Mexico, he wanted to conquer this impressive city, with its striking architecture and a massive number of Aztec warriors. The last Aztec ruler, Montezuma II, lived there.

The typical Aztec household consisted of a husband, wife, their unmarried children, and the husband's relatives. Women mainly tended to the household and the children. Everyone had a job to do, even the youths. Many times the work involved creating goods—including tools, pottery, baskets, and figurines—to sell or trade. They sent valuable goods down the Gulf Coast and into the area now known as Guatemala. There, the valuables were traded. In addition to objects, valuable goods included natural resources such as gold and salt. The Aztecs traded these items for tropical bird feathers, cacao beans, rubber, and more.

The Spaniards incorporated many Nahuatl words into their language. Later, these words entered English as well. They include: "coyote," "chili," "chocolate," "avocado," and "guacamole."

Most Aztecs relied on farming as their primary means of sustenance. Their main crop was maize, or corn, but they also grew beans. Since their farmland tended to be in arid climates, they developed complex irrigation systems to maintain their crops. They also used fertilizer and even learned to farm in swampy areas by creating a type of floating garden.

When Aztec women became pregnant, people respected and revered them, as the Aztecs viewed pregnancy as a gift from the gods. The Aztecs cared for pregnant women and prohibited them from lifting heavy objects or doing strenuous work. Married to a chief, Malinalli's mother must have received an enormous amount of care while pregnant.

This Mexican engraving, made in 1885, is what Malinche, interpreter and concubine of Hernán Cortés, might have looked like. The artwork hangs in a library in Spain.

Since Malinalli's family was prestigious, she may have had some formal education. Girls rarely received an education beyond how to tend house or make blankets and cloth. Weaving was a key skill for women, and girls sometimes faced harsh judgment concerning their work as weavers. That Malinalli received any education at all probably meant that she had won her father's favor. The lessons Malinalli received may have helped her when she served as Cortés's interpreter.[2]

Most Aztec children did not receive any real education until age five. What they studied depended on their social status. They may have learned about good manners and how to properly demonstrate them. The more privileged Aztecs likely received a more well-rounded education. Their excellence in astronomy, geometry, architecture, and other fields continue to awe scholars today.

Unfortunately, Malinalli's education couldn't save her from the events that turned her life upside down. Her father died when she was still a young girl. Afraid to lose her status in their tribe, Malinalli's mother quickly remarried another nobleman and gave birth to a son. She decided to give Malinalli's inheritance to the boy. She handed over Malinalli to traders as if the girl were a slave. The Aztecs did not normally banish their children, particularly young girls, in this manner, so Malinalli's mother pretended she'd died to avoid judgment from her community. She even held a mock funeral and burial for her daughter.[3]

Malinalli's destiny was sealed when the wandering traders headed west and sold her to the ruling chief of Tabasco, on the Yucatán coast. This new tribe spoke a Mayan dialect and so the young girl, who spoke and understood Nahuatl, eventually learned the Mayan dialect as well. This would prove to be an invaluable skill that may have saved her life or, at the very least, prevented her from living as a common slave.

Malinalli would later learn a third language.

Tabasco

Destiny, fate, or coincidence brought Hernán Cortés and La Malinche together for the first time in an area known as Tabasco, Mexico. Most Americans know Tabasco as a type of hot sauce. The sauce may bear the name of the Mexican state, but it has nothing to do with Mexico. In fact, the sauce was actually created in the United States, where it is manufactured as well.

Located in southeastern Mexico, Tabasco is one of thirty-one states and thirty-two federal entities that make up the country. Cortés and his expedition sailed to Tabasco, which borders Guatemala to the south.

There are several stories about how the area came to be called Tabasco. Spanish conquistador Bernal Díaz del Castillo mentions in his memoir that the name comes from one of the local rivers. But both the Maya and Aztecs say the name originates from their language and refers to a lord or ruler.

Firsthand Accounts of Malinalli

Spanish conquistador Bernal Díaz del Castillo wrote in his memoirs that Malinalli was the most striking, in both appearance and manner, of the twenty women given to Cortés and his men. Díaz del Castillo finished writing about his experiences as a conquistador about fifty years after he'd retired from the battlefield. Born in 1490, he died in 1584, living nearly a century. Díaz del Castillo's writings were later compiled and published as a memoir. They provided one of the earliest accounts of Cortés's exploits in Mexico and his interactions with Malinalli.

Díaz del Castillo described Malinalli as someone who could not be compared to the other nineteen women presented as "gifts." Times were very different in the sixteenth century. Today, of course, the idea that a human being could be bestowed upon another as a gift is morally objectionable, although human trafficking remains a problem across the globe. Although Malinalli was trafficked into slavery, Díaz del Castillo still saw her value as a human being. He described her as "a very fine woman." More specifically, he characterized her as "a lady of distinction, the daughter of a powerful chief and a princess who had subjects of her, which, indeed, you might see from her appearance." In addition to her physical beauty, Díaz del Castillo said she was the most active and lively of the women in her group.[4]

Clearly, Malinalli stood out as a woman of distinction who never lost the regal manner of someone born into nobility. But it's uncertain whether she was indeed beautiful or just had distinct physical characteristics because she did not belong to the same ethnic group as the other women. We'll never know.

Historians know little about Malinalli's life after her mother sold her into slavery and faked her death. Incredibly, she and Cortés would encounter her mother and half-brother years later.[5] (We'll discuss that in greater detail shortly.) As a young female slave, Malinalli may have been subjected to horrific abuse—mental, physical, and sexual in nature. She may have learned to appease her "owners" as best she could and behaved similarly when given to Cortés.

Despite her ascension from slave girl to Cortés's interpreter and the role she played in Mexico's conquest, Cortés only mentioned her twice in his letters to Spain's king. Her absence from these letters is especially remarkable, given that Malinalli was far more than his interpreter but the mother of his child as well. In one letter, Cortés does not bother to mention

Bernal Díaz del Castillo

Historians have relied upon Bernal Díaz del Castillo's memoirs to document and understand how the Spanish—and in particular Hernán Cortés and his band of soldiers—conquered Mexico. Since Díaz del Castillo belonged to Cortés's group, he provided firsthand accounts of Mexico's conquest.

The soldier and writer was born circa 1490 in Medina del Campo in Spain. He grew up in a poor family and received very little formal education. From a young age, he set off to make his fortune by becoming a soldier and joining the expeditions to the Americas.

He traveled to what is now Panama. Later he took part in the conquest and settling of Cuba. Díaz del Castillo joined Cortés on his expedition to Mexico and kept notes that drew upon his many conversations with other soldiers about their experiences. It was not uncommon for soldiers to write of their conquests, often glorifying their efforts in a bid to seek reward.

Díaz del Castillo was no exception. Thus, he surely wrote his highly cited work with his own best interests in mind.

Malinalli by name. Instead, he refers to her only as the "Indian interpreter."[6] This oversight may stem from Cortés's desire to take all of the credit for conquering Mexico. But it also shows how little women, especially indigenous women, were valued during this time.

While Cortés saw fit to overlook Malinalli, Díaz del Castillo and Tenochtitlan ruler Andrés de Tapia Motelchiuhtzin filled in some of the missing pieces. Motelchiuhtzin even mentions Malinalli's background and childhood in his writing. He recalled:

"Of the twenty Indian women that had been given him, the marqués had divided some among certain gentlemen … one of the women spoke to them, so we found she spoke two languages and our Spanish interpreter could understand her. We learned from her that as a child she had been stolen by some traders and taken to be sold in the land of Tabasco where she was brought up."[7]

Although he says that traders stole Malinalli, most other accounts say that her mother committed the unthinkable—she sold the young girl. Moreover, many accounts note that the women given to Cortés and his men were handed over to them as sex slaves and domestic servants to grind maize and make tortillas. Other accounts suggest that the Spaniards may have treated these women with a certain degree of dignity, especially Malinalli. In any case, the women were "property" with no control over their lives and bodies. Today, forced sexual contact between one person and another is considered sexual assault or rape. Sexual assault remains a major concern in the twenty-first century, and a number of laws, organizations, and activists work to fight this terrible problem.

PARTNERSHIP

Hernán Cortés had a problem, but that was nothing new for him. He had already surmounted a number of obstacles. He overcame poor health as a child to become a world traveler and soldier. He overcame his own immaturities to finally take hold of his dreams. He overcame the lack of a college degree to put himself in a position to succeed.

To Conquer or Convert?

Cortés also defied Velázquez and headed to Mexico with a small fleet of ships and a loyal band of men. As a result of his efforts, he found himself in a strange land with unfamiliar customs, not to mention a massive and powerful Aztec army. Cortés needed to decide if he should make peace with the Aztecs or attempt to conquer them.

His inability to speak indigenous languages made determining his next move difficult. The powerful Aztecs spoke Nahuatl. Cortés spoke Spanish. His main interpreter until then spoke Spanish and Mayan. Cortés had to overcome the language barrier. The slave girl Malinalli, fluent in Nahuatl and a Mayan dialect, could help him do just that.

Cortés decided that he would speak Spanish to his interpreter Aguilar, who, in turn, would relay the message in Mayan to Malinalli. Then, she would translate it into Nahuatl, speaking with the Aztecs on Cortés's behalf. Before Cortés's ambitious language project took off, however, he wanted to convert the native women to Christianity. Aguilar, a priest, spoke to them about no longer worshipping Mayan or Aztec gods. He told them their idols were evil and that Christianity was the religion of the one true God.

He proceeded to baptize them to make them "born again." The ceremony required that the women get new names. Malinalli became Marina in honor of the Virgin Mary, mother of Jesus. She and the others baptized likely became the first Christian women in the land the Spaniards called New Spain.[1]

Marina then became instrumental in convincing other natives to give up their indigenous religions and convert to Christianity. It's unclear if she truly believed in Christ or simply realized that anyone who did not comply and convert would suffer under Spanish rule. Marina's efforts to spread Christianity did not go unnoticed. Before long, the Spanish gave her the title Doña, reserved for the most revered and respected women. This title signaled that Marina had become an important and trusted member of the group.

Her value as an interpreter and an emissary, or ambassador, was evident from the start. Interpreting the words of Cortés and Aguilar, she convinced Aztec tribal chiefs, leaders, and members to swear their allegiance to Spain and the church. This was not an easy task. Cortés had to convince the indigenous peoples he'd just defeated in battle that he was not a god to be feared and revered. Rather, he served the Crown. When they understood this, they swore their allegiance to Spain, becoming the first native Mexicans to do so.

This 1825 drawing captures the moment when Hernán Cortés met his interpreter Gerónimo de Aguilar. The Maya enslaved Aguilar for eight years.

This illustration is a copy of one of the few historical Aztec accounts that survived Spanish rule, the Codex Telleriano-Remensis of 1540. It shows Spaniards and Aztecs battling.

Cortés could not have accomplished this feat without the help of his new interpreter, Doña Marina. But Cortés wanted more. He set out to claim all of the land, and its gold, for Spain. He could only do so if the fearsome Aztec Empire submitted to him in its entirety or crumbled in battle.

On Easter Sunday 1519, Cortés and his group reached an area known as San Juan de Ulúa. The Aztec ruler Montezuma II had been keeping tabs on Cortés and knew his movements well. He sent several men and two trusted governors to greet the Spaniards. They exchanged gifts, including an ornate chair that Cortés explained was for Montezuma II. The conquistador said that he would love to meet the ruler and see him sit in the chair.[2]

Marina interpreted for the two factions. Cortés made a show of force by riding his horse in full battle gear and ordering the canon to be fired. The Aztecs had never seen or heard this weapon, so it probably frightened and intimidated them. Cortés may have put on a powerful show, with Marina's help, but the Aztec governors still rebuffed him. They would not let him meet with Montezuma II.

The Aztec leader tried to bribe and buy off the Spaniards. He would send gold and other precious resources as gifts, but his efforts seemingly backfired. The gold only made Cortés and his men more eager to see Montezuma II in person and, in all likelihood, seize whatever gold they could.[4] Cortés continued to move inland, conquering small towns or coercing—with Marina's help—the inhabitants to side with him and not Montezuma. He hadn't openly declared war against Montezuma II, but Cortés learned which groups disliked the Aztec ruler. This helped him form alliances and allegiances.

As time went on, Doña Marina, an intelligent woman, quickly picked up the Castilian Spanish dialect. Eventually, Cortés no longer needed Aguilar.

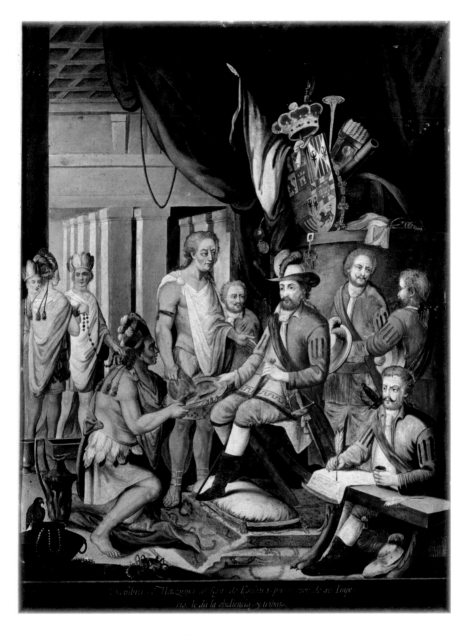

Aztec ruler Montezuma II offered gifts of gold to Hernán Cortés. Notice how the artist depicts Montezuma kneeling before the Spaniard.

Montezuma II

Sometimes referred to as Moctezuma II or Montezuma the Young, this Aztec ruler was the ninth leader of the Aztec Empire and ruled over the vast realm from 1502-1520.

His legacy, much like the legacies of Cortés and Marina, is complicated. Some paint him as a weak-willed, indecisive ruler whose actions led to the fall of the Aztec Empire. Others say he was willing to work with the Spanish invaders.

Either way, he was very superstitious, mainly worshipped two Aztec gods, regularly sacrificed humans to the gods, and had dozens of lovers and hundreds of children.

He was the first indigenous ruler of Mexico to have contact with Europeans, and for centuries historians have debated why he didn't do more to defend his empire. Many say his poor decisions will forever mark him as the leader of a fallen nation.

But many historical accounts are so biased in nature that it is difficult to ascertain what kind of ruler Montezuma was and whether his actions really did cause the fall of an empire.[3]

New Allies

As Cortés made his way to Montezuma II and the Aztec capital, he gained resources and allies. In particular, the people of Tlaxcala, known as Tlaxcalans, sided with the conquistador after losing several battles to him. A free state, Tlaxcala did not live under Aztec rule, but the residents distrusted Cortés and any outside forces. Initially, they fought the Spaniards before realizing they could not defeat an army with horses, a cannon, and armor.

The Aztec archaeological site of Calixtlahuaca housed the Temple of Tlaloc and Altar of Skulls (or Tzompantli), believed to have been built in the fourteenth century.

The City of Cholula

Cholula was undoubtedly one of the Aztec Empire's most important cities by the time Hernán Cortés and Marina arrived there. It is also the city where Marina proved her worth and loyalty to Cortés, all of the Spaniards on the expedition, and the Spanish Crown alike.

In the sixteenth century, the city boasted a population of more than one hundred thousand. A vibrant and busy marketplace, people visited from all over to trade there. The city had also earned a reputation for fine craftsmanship and the production of high-quality goods to trade, especially pottery.

But the native Mexicans best knew the Aztec city as a religious center with a pyramid. Known as the Temple of Tlaloc, it is the largest pyramid built by an ancient culture and larger than the more well-known pyramids of Egypt.[5] The people of Cholula worshipped the ancient god Quetzalcóatl, previously worshipped by the Olmec and Toltec civilizations.

> *Egypt is famous for its pyramids, but the Aztec, Olmec, Maya, and Inca peoples built the amazing structures as well. The Americas contain more pyramids than Egypt does.*

The Tlaxcalans ultimately welcomed Cortés, with Marina relaying the conquistador's intentions to their leader. Cortés would not stop moving his forces inland until he met Montezuma II. The Tlaxcalans believed they had finally encountered a fighting force that, combined with theirs, might topple the Aztec Empire.

During this time, the Mexican natives began to use the name "Malinche." However, they used it to describe Cortés rather than Marina herself. The word means "Marina's Captain," since he and the young woman were rarely apart. Over time, "Malinche" evolved into "La Malinche."

With La Malinche and the Tlaxcalans in his court, Cortés pressed on. The next big city that stood between the Spaniard and the Aztec capital of Tenochtitlan was Cholula. Rather than stopping the Spaniards from closing in, Montezuma II sent word through his emissaries that Cortés and his men would be welcomed into the city should they choose to enter it. Montezuma II guaranteed their safety even as the Tlaxcalans, via La Malinche, urged Cortés not to listen to him.

They said the Aztecs there would surely ambush the Spaniards before they ever reached Montezuma II.[6] Cortés ignored their advice and proceeded to enter Cholula. An expertly played game of cat and mouse followed, with La Malinche working as a double agent of sorts. Her efforts saved Cortés and his men from catastrophe.

LA MALINCHE TO THE RESCUE

Hernán Cortés's defeat and takeover of Cholula paved the way for the Spanish to conquer and colonize Mexico. But a number of sources argue that the Cholula battle was more of a massacre than a fair fight. This bloody episode also stands out as the moment when La Malinche appeared to forsake her Mexican heritage and firmly pledge her allegiance to Cortés and Spain.

Trapped in Cholula

When Cortés and the rest of the Spaniards entered Cholula in October 1519, the magnificent city's architectural wonders, impressive temples, busy marketplace, and organization wowed them. The buildings were strong and well built. A group of Cholulans greeted the Spanish but insisted the fierce Tlaxcalan warriors remain outside the city gates.

Over the course of a few days, however, the Cholulans grew cool toward the Spanish. They wanted them to leave. They stopped bringing Cortés and his men food, and the city's leaders and elders refused to meet with the conqueror.[1]

Remnants of this Cholula pyramid are still visible today in the foothills below Our Lady of Remedies church. The Spaniards left Cholula to meet Aztec leader Montezuma II.

During this time, rumors that the Cholulans were planning an ambush reached Cortés. His men said the Cholulans had barricaded streets and placed boulders on rooftops to ambush them. Cortés refused to believe the rumors until it came from a source he trusted—La Malinche.

She'd befriended a Cholulan woman during her brief time there, a wife of a cacique, or nobleman. They began to see each other regularly and struck up quite the friendship. According to the most detailed account, written by Díaz del Castillo, La Malinche only got acquainted with the woman to learn about any Cholulan plots against Cortés and his force. The women became so friendly that the nobleman's wife even offered La Malinche a way to escape from Cortés and marry her son.

Díaz del Castillo wrote that La Malinche never took the offer seriously but made the woman believe the plan interested her to further win her trust. He writes that La Malinche went so far as to call the woman "mother" to ingratiate herself to her. Acting as a double agent, she "agreed" to marry the woman's son and betray her Spanish captors.

"I don't want them to notice us, so Mother you wait here while I begin to bring my property," La Malinche purportedly told the unsuspecting woman. "And then we will be able to go."[2]

But instead of leaving with them, La Malinche turned the woman over to Cortés, allowing him to learn about the plot against him. Supposedly, Montezuma II had twenty thousand warriors lying in wait to kill the Spanish invaders. The leader of the Aztec Empire reportedly had visions that the Spaniards would end his reign and decided to do everything he could to keep that from happening. Montezuma hadn't counted on La Malinche to spoil his plans.

Her actions impressed Cortés so much that he mentioned them to the Spanish rulers in a letter describing the Cholulan plot. Some historians have speculated that there was no plot to kill the conquistadors at all and that La Malinche simply concocted the story to curry favor with the Spanish. But others have refuted those theories, since a number of people around at the time documented the plot.

Aware of the ambush scheme, Cortés realized that his life was in danger whether he remained in Cholula or tried to leave. His options appeared severely limited. But Cortés had previously found a way to overcome insurmountable odds. Cholula would be no different.

The Cholula Massacre

Cortés first convinced two very trusted Cholulan holy men to visit. He told them that he planned to leave the city the following day and needed two thousand men to help him carry his goods. He also wanted all the noblemen assembled so that he could thank them for their incredible hospitality.[3]

He then sent word of the ambush to his allies, the Tlaxcalan warriors outside the city gates. He told them to listen for the first gunshot and then come in to help his cause. He warned them to wear green wreaths on their heads so that his men would not mistake them for Cholulans. They did not want to kill them by mistake.[4]

Cortés and his men spent the night fearing the ambush would come early. He posted many guards, and every man slept with his weapon. Many got no sleep at all. They felt relief at the sight of the sunrise.

As day broke, Cortés and his men gathered in the town square, weapons drawn. The Cholulans came to greet them, as promised. And Cortés came right out and told them that he knew of their treachery against him.

The Cholulans were a very superstitious people. They felt thunderstruck that Cortés knew of their plan. They took it as a

The Tlaxcalans

Hernán Cortés greatly benefited from his alliance with the Tlaxcalans. These fierce warriors provided his forces with enough manpower to topple the mighty Aztec Empire. But who exactly were the Tlaxcalans?

A Tlaxcalan warrior pulls Hernán Cortés from a canal and onto his boat. The Tlaxcalans allied themselves with Cortés, giving him a formidable fighting force.

They were an indigenous group of Nahua heritage. They lived in Tlaxcala and spoke three different languages: Nahuatl, Otami, and Pinome. Never conquered by the Aztecs, these powerful warriors lived in the empire in a free and independent state. Because of their alliance with the Spaniards, they enjoyed benefits that other indigenous Mexicans did not. The conquistadors allowed them to carry guns, ride horses, own land, and even hold titles of nobility.

They mainly settled in northern Mexico, where the Spanish allowed them to rule themselves.

very bad sign. They wondered if he could read minds. Was he a god? They simply did not know what to do.

Too stunned to deny their deceit, they blamed Montezuma II and said he had coerced them to do it. Cortés told them that was no excuse to backstab him, since he'd only tried to convert them to Christianity and stop them from worshipping idols. In his memoirs, Díaz del Castillo quoted Cortés's address to the stunned crowd of Cholulans in the town square.

> *"How anxious these traitors are to see us among the ravines so that they can gorge themselves on our flesh. But our lord will prevent it."*

"How anxious these traitors are to see us among the ravines so that they can gorge themselves on our flesh. But our lord will prevent it," [5] he said.

He then ordered his men to fire upon the crowd, striking many noblemen dead at once and signaling the fierce Tlaxcalans to enter the city and join the attack. Cortés's men went into the crowd of thousands and slaughtered the mainly unarmed noblemen and priests who had gathered. It was a massacre.

The Spaniards plundered the city and took all the gold they could. They slaughtered animals and knocked down temples. An incensed Cortés allowed the Tlaxcalans to sack the city, take slaves, and continue the massacre. They destroyed the city of Cholula.

After the Spanish spent days killing and plundering, some of the noblemen who escaped reentered the city. Cortés let them live on two conditions: they had to swear allegiance to Spain and warn others about the consequences of crossing the Spanish. Clearly, the men had no choice but to agree to

This 1698 painting by Miguel González illustrates how Spanish conquerors, led by Hernán Cortés, mercilessly massacred the Cholulans. An alleged Cholulan conspiracy plot against him enraged Cortés.

Human Sacrifice

Montezuma II used human sacrifice to appease the gods and gain favor. Whenever he felt that the Spanish invaders were threatening his empire, he would increase the number of sacrifices.

This was not a new concept.

Human sacrifice originated in ancient civilizations that predate the Aztecs. The ancient Chinese and Japanese practiced such killings. Some stories say the Great Wall of China contains thousands of sacrificed victims. Homer's classic tale about the Trojan War, *The Odyssey*, even mentions human sacrifice. That epic poem dates back to about 800 BCE.

Regardless of the method of human sacrifice or the culture, the goal was always the same: to gain favor from some deity. When the head of the household died, ethnic groups such as the ancient Egyptians would sacrifice residents, usually servants. They believed this allowed the servants to continue caring for their master in the afterlife.

Over time, societies began to disapprove of human sacrifice. People turned to animal sacrifice instead, although this practice also raises moral questions.

these conditions if they wanted to live. Having massacred the townspeople and left Cholula in ruins, Cortés helped some of the survivors rebuild their homes and reopen the marketplace. The Spaniards then took to the road again.

Montezuma II now feared the Spanish more than ever. He sent word that he would pay tribute to the Spanish Crown if he could avoid a personal meeting with Cortés. He increased his number of human sacrifices, hoping it would please his gods and keep the Spaniards from coming. He also sent even more gold to Cortés in an effort to keep him away and buy him off. To appease Cortés, the panicked Aztec leader sent word that the Cholulan people had acted on their own and that he had nothing to do with any planned attack.[6]

At this point, nothing stood in Cortés's way as he headed to meet Montezuma II.

CORTÉS MEETS MONTEZUMA II

Ever the strategist, Hernán Cortés did not leave Cholula for Tenochtitlan until he made sure the Cholulans and Tlaxcalans had formed an alliance. Since La Malinche could interpret for him, Cortés turned to her for help in uniting the two groups. Using La Malinche as his mouthpiece, the Spaniard got the Cholulans and Tlaxcalans to put their past grievances behind them and forge a new bond. Given how Cortés and his forces had savagely destroyed Cholula, the remaining Cholulans likely felt that they had to team up with the Tlaxcalans to please the conquistador. They were left powerless.

Journey to Tenochtitlan

For Cortés, getting the Cholulans to help was vital. He did not know what to expect when he reached Tenochtitlan and wanted a place where he and his troops could safely retreat if necessary. Montezuma II had a massive army, and Cortés and his forces should have been no match.

In November, Cortés and his men finally made their way to Montezuma. Along the way, with the help of La Malinche,

This seventeenth-century painting hangs in the Franz Mayer Museum in Mexico City, Mexico. It shows the clashes between the Aztec warriors and the conquering Spaniards.

Cortés's forces continued to grow. The members of just about every village, tribe, outpost, or settlement they encountered agreed to form an alliance with Cortés. They resented Montezuma II's endless need for tribute and humans to sacrifice. They joined in the march toward Tenochtitlan. Although many of these Mexican natives feared Montezuma II, they'd tired of his oppressive reign. They wanted change.[1]

They believed that Montezuma II wielded a special magical power within the walls of Tenochtitlan. They warned Cortés not to enter the city because they feared he would fall under Montezuma's spell. In reality, the Spaniards would have to take care not to let the Aztec ruler's gold mesmerize them.

The ominous signs and potential threats did not faze Cortés, and he continued his long trek toward the Aztec capital. Fearful of what awaited them, his men fell into despair as they neared Tenochtitlan. They received word that Montezuma had barricaded all the roads except for one with large boulders and fallen trees. The barricades meant that the Spanish invaders would not surprise the Aztec emperor.

During the journey to meet Montezuma, Cortés tried to lift his men's spirits. He laughed with them and told funny stories. He reportedly did not sleep and spent the nights with his sentinels guarding the caravan.

By this time, Montezuma II was sick with worry. He believed angry gods had sent the Spaniards to destroy his kingdom. He called his advisers and asked them for their counsel. Some told him to welcome Cortés with open arms as a prince or foreign dignitary. Others urged him to send his forces at once to cut down the Spaniards before they ever set foot in his great city.[4]

But fear paralyzed Montezuma II. He could not decide what to do, so he sent another emissary to greet Cortés and bring him gifts. Then he decided to greet Cortés himself. Montezuma ordered his many noblemen to adorn themselves in their finest clothes to impress the visiting Spaniards. The emperor headed north in a magnificent royal caravan. His own personal vehicle, carried by servants, was adorned with gold and colorful feathers. It made quite the sight.[5]

Finally, the two parties came within sight of each other. Montezuma II left his caravan and walked along a carpet that servants laid out in front of him so that his feet would never touch the ground. Cortés himself dismounted and rushed over to greet this impressive leader. He thanked Montezuma II for the gifts and even placed a necklace around the leader's neck. He would have embraced Montezuma II, but the emperor's noblemen and guards stopped him. The Aztecs did not consider a hug befitting of an emperor.[6]

With the help of his trusted interpreter La Malinche, Cortés told Montezuma II that he was overjoyed to finally meet such a great leader. He said he felt honored to meet with him. In turn, the Aztecs found La Malinche impressive because she could communicate with both them and the Spaniards. They believed her to be very special and trusted her as a result. This gave her great power over them, and some historians have wondered whether she relayed Cortés's exact words to them or put her own twist on the conversation.

When Cortés finished speaking, Montezuma II turned to Malinche, who translated the Aztec leader's words into Spanish. Montezuma II returned Cortés's praise and said he likewise felt honored to meet the conquistador. He then ordered two of his nephews, who were great and powerful lords in their own right, to accompany the Spaniards.[7]

Prisoners or Guests?

The meeting had gone so well that excitement had replaced the fear both groups felt. Montezuma II welcomed Cortés and

Tenochtitlan

The Aztec capital was on an island near the western shore of Lake Texcoco. Home to two hundred thousand people, it operated as both a cultural and religious center. Its importance to the Aztecs cannot be overstated. Founded in 1345, the city included a large pyramid called Temple Mayor, which honored the Aztec gods of Huitzilopochtli and Tlaloc.[2]

Three causeways with removable bridges connected Tenochtitlan to the mainland. This protected the glorious city from the threat of attack. The ceremonial precinct at the heart of the city was walled off and protected by guards as well. The religious center also contained the emperor's palace. The gladiator's stone sat directly in front of the Temple Mayor. There, people to be sacrificed were chained up before meeting their fate at the hands of a soldier or priest. [3]

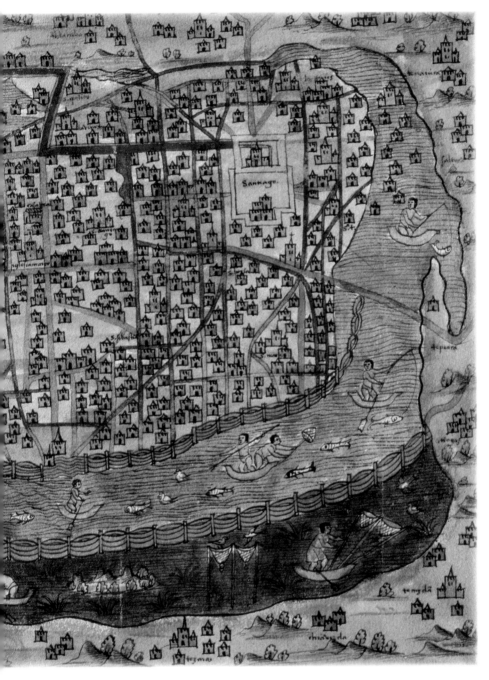

This 1560 map shows the island of Tenochtitlan, once deemed the most important island in the world. Tenochtitlan was the capital of the Aztec Empire and ruler Montezuma II.

his men, and they traveled along one of the open causeways to the capital. There, the Aztec emperor received them as honored dignitaries.

According to Díaz del Castillo, Montezuma II was an impressive sight. He wrote one of the only descriptions of the leader:

> "The great Montezuma II was about forty years old, of good height, well proportioned, spare and slight, and not very dark, though of the usual Indian complexion. He did not wear his hair long but just over his ears, and he had a short black beard, well-shaped and thin. His face was rather long and cheerful, he had fine eyes, and in his appearance and manner could express geniality or, when necessary, a serious composure. He was very neat and clean, and took a bath every afternoon." [8]

The next morning, Cortés sent word to Montezuma II that he intended to visit him in the palace, along with a few of his men. The request surprised the Aztecs, as guests very rarely entered the palace. But the emperor greeted them and with La Malinche's help, the two leaders had a conversation. Díaz del Castillo recalled that after a small amount of pleasantries, Cortés told Montezuma about his hopes to convert the Aztecs to Christianity.

He urged Montezuma and his men to give up their gods and instead embrace Christianity and "the one true

"His face was rather long and cheerful, he had fine eyes, and in his appearance and manner could express geniality or, when necessary, a serious composure."

Hernán Cortés told Montezuma the story of Adam and Eve to convert him to Christianity. This nineteenth-century illustration shows the pair's expulsion from the Garden of Eden.

God." He told the emperor that the gods the Aztecs worshipped were not gods at all, but evil. Cortés even said they looked ugly.[9] The conquistador then spoke briefly about Adam and Eve and Christianity's version of man's origin. He spoke of Jesus Christ and the suffering he endured.

Montezuma II listened patiently and thanked Cortés when he finished speaking. He told the Spaniard that he didn't doubt the Christian god had served him well. Still, he believed in the Aztec gods and would not be converted.[10] Cortés seemed satisfied that he had done his Christian duty and at least tried to convert Montezuma II. The two men remained friendly.

Aztec Weaponry

Bernal Díaz del Castillo wrote of a building near Montezuma II's palace filled with every weapon imaginable. He described the wonderful craftsmanship of the weapons and how many were made of silver, gold, and encrusted precious stones. Warriors who'd proven themselves in battle received a higher rank in the Aztec military. The higher the rank, the more ornate and spectacular their garb and weaponry.

The Aztec fighters' main weapons included long-range spears. They stood nearly 6 feet (1.8 meters) and could be thrown from a great distance. The weapons also included large bows and arrows to strike an enemy down from afar. Most warriors also possessed a sling and a pouch of rocks. This helped them to severely wound opponents in armor. Finally, the Aztecs carried a melee club for close combat.

The blowgun Aztecs used to shoot poison-tipped darts into the flesh of their enemies stood out as their most interesting weapon. The warriors extracted the poison from the secretions of the numerous poisonous tree frogs that lived in the area.[11]

The Spaniards stayed in Tenochtitlan as Montezuma's honored guests for several weeks. The ruler allowed them to build a small Christian chapel where they could worship. There, the conquistadors would meet and discuss their growing anxieties. Relations between the Aztecs and them had changed. The Spaniards felt more like prisoners than guests.

They believed Montezuma II and his tremendous army would kill them. They feared the servants, who cooled toward them, would poison them. But they felt trapped. Surely Montezuma II would order them killed if they tried to leave, and surely his forces would rise up and kill them should anything happen to their leader. They devised a plot to lure Montezuma to their quarters, where they could control his every move. They would threaten to kill him if he warned his people about their plans. But neither the Spaniards nor Montezuma II realized how big of a role La Malinche would play in the events that followed.

THE FALL OF THE AZTEC EMPIRE

The seeds of the plot germinated throughout the night as Cortés and his men prayed about what to do. They stayed up all night in prayer with one hand on their weapons for fear that Montezuma II would come for them.

Montezuma Folds

He did not, and in the morning Cortés dispatched his plan. He would go to the palace with La Malinche and a few of his officers. Just like before, he would send word beforehand so as not to surprise the emperor.

After their normal greetings and salutations, Cortés unleashed a blistering verbal attack on Montezuma II, saying that he was well aware that the Aztec leader ordered the attack on his men in Cholula and had played a role in the skirmishes they had been involved in during their journey to the capital. He told Montezuma that he had betrayed them and that the Spanish had only come in peace.

Then, he made Montezuma II the following offer:

"However, notwithstanding all this treachery, I will refrain from making war upon you, which would only end in the total destruction of this city. But in order that peace may be maintained between us, you must make a small sacrifice, which is, to follow us quietly into our quarters, and take up your abode there. There you will receive the same attention, and be treated with the same respect as if you were in your own palace. But if you make any alarm now, or call out to your attendants, you are a dead man."[1]

This 1550 illustration shows La Malinche interpreting for Hernán Cortés as Montezuma presents the Spaniard with gifts of gold and women.

> *"I will refrain from making war upon you."*
> — La Malinche

But Montezuma II continued to deny that he was behind the attacks and refused to go. The impasse lasted more than thirty minutes until some of the soldiers began to yell and suggest killing him. Montezuma turned to La Malinche and asked her to tell him what the soldiers had said. Instead, according to Díaz del Castillo, she urged the monarch to go peacefully with them. He continued to refuse and offered his children as hostages.

But La Malinche strongly pressed him to comply. "Great monarch, if I may be allowed to give you advice, make no further difficulties, but immediately follow them to their quarters," she said. "I am confident they will pay you every respect, and treat you as becomes a powerful monarch. But if you continue to refuse, they will cut you down on the spot."[2]

Montezuma II, ashamed and feeling the sting of defeat, went with them. His people gathered in the streets, ready to pounce and attack the small Spanish group, but the emperor raised his hand and assured them that he'd decided to go with them. As the months passed, Montezuma II suffered more indignities at the hands of Cortés and his officers. But Cortés openly punished any of his men who acted rudely toward the emperor.

Each indignity broke Montezuma II down. On one occasion, Cortés even had shackles put on the emperor's feet while he ordered one of the Aztec generals burned alive for attacking the Spaniards months before. Montezuma II wept, as did his servants. They could not understand how their great ruler had lost power so quickly.[3]

This painting shows Cortés ordering shackles to be placed on Montezuma II's ankles. Montezuma did not recover from this humiliation. He lost the respect of the Aztecs as well.

Every morning, Cortés would tell the imprisoned ruler what he wanted him to do. Montezuma II would greet the people from a balcony as he had before his imprisonment and would implement Cortés's orders as if they were his own. Cortés was essentially ruling the Aztec Empire.

Cortés took more and more liberties as time passed. He even planted a huge wooden cross at the top of the pyramid that overlooked the area where human sacrifices had taken place. Life began changing for the Aztecs. The human sacrifices stopped, and the people rarely saw Montezuma. The emperor had lost his zeal for life, and the people could see that he was unhappy.

Meanwhile, another coup of sorts was taking place. The noblemen in Montezuma II's palace now fully understood that their ruler was nothing more than a puppet for the Spanish invaders. They whispered about how to seize power back from Montezuma II, or, rather, Cortés.

But greed intervened. Cortés and some of his men left the Aztec capital city to go on an expedition. Back in Tenochtitlan, one of his captains, Pedro de Alvarado, ordered the Spaniards to attack several unarmed Aztec noblemen celebrating a religious feast. Alvarado had also behaved cruelly toward the indigenous people when the conquistadors first landed in Cozumel. After the attack, the conquistadors stole the jewels and valuables the Aztecs were wearing.

The Aztecs Revolt

The attack enraged the Aztecs as well as Cortés when he received the news. He headed back to Tenochtitlan, fearful that he and his men would face a full Aztec rebellion.[4] He returned just as a battle broke out in the capital. Cortés was angry with Alvarado and even more so with himself for leaving such an irresponsible person in charge of a very delicate situation. But he could not dole out punishments just yet. He had to fight to survive.

Miraculously, Cortés and his men reached their quarters unscathed. But before long, they heard the angry murmur of thousands of Aztecs approaching. American historian William H. Prescott described the Aztec attack. He wrote:

William H. Prescott

William H. Prescott is one of the most translated historians in modern history. In 1796, he was born in Salem, Massachusetts, home of the infamous witch trials of the seventeenth century. He suffered from numerous health issues, most notably involving his eyes. His near blindness frequently prevented him from reading or writing by himself. He often needed assistance.

However, Prescott was blessed with an eidetic memory, commonly known as a photographic memory. He only had to glance at something for a few seconds before memorizing it. In the early 1820s, Prescott, a Harvard graduate who traveled throughout Europe, learned about Spain's history. He found it fascinating. He especially took interest in the Spanish Empire's sudden decline after its short but glorious tenure as a world superpower.

Although he wrote about Cortés three hundred years after Mexico's conquest, Prescott was a master of using archived accounts to piece together a comprehensive history. He took care not to merely repeat hearsay or rumor. Instead, he searched and investigated recorded accounts.

He died in 1859.

"As they drew near the enclosure, the Aztecs set up a hideous yell, or rather that shrill whistle used in fight by the nations of Anahuac, which rose far above the sound of shell and atabal, and their other rude instruments of warlike melody. They followed this by a tempest of missiles—stones, darts and arrows—which fell thick as rain on the besieged, while volleys of the same kind descended from the crowded terraces in the neighborhood."[5]

The Aztecs continued their siege on the Spanish quarters, but their arrows and rocks did little damage. The building was made of stone, and the soldiers wore armor. So, the Aztecs tried a new tactic. They scaled the palace's walls and engaged the invaders in hand-to-hand combat. The battle lasted all day, and many died. Aware that the Aztecs would return the next day in larger numbers, the Spaniards decided to leave the palace and launch a surprise attack on their foes in the morning.

Using cannons and horses, the Spaniards unleashed a vicious and brutal attack on their rivals. But the Aztecs simply retreated and waited for Cortés and his men to go back into their quarters. Then they attacked again.

This time, several Aztecs made it over the wall. Cortés feared the warriors would quickly overtake them. He was out of options. He needed help from the man he'd imprisoned and humiliated—Montezuma II.

Cortés enlisted La Malinche to assure Montezuma II that he and his men wanted to leave peacefully. They just needed the ruler to ensure their safe passage out of Tenochtitlan. A shell of the man he once was, Montezuma wanted no part of Cortés's plan but ultimately agreed to it.

The emperor dressed in full regalia and went to the balcony. There was a hush below as the attacking Aztecs recognized their leader. The people bowed and knelt in reverence as Montezuma

The Spaniards took the regal Montezuma II prisoner. He would never live again as a free man. The decisions he made leading up to his downfall remain puzzling.

La Malinche's Revenge?

Historians do not know what motivated La Malinche during the Mexican conquest. Did she behave as she did in order to stay alive, or did she truly believe in Christ and want the Mexican natives to follow suit? It's unclear if she thought her people would benefit from Spanish rule or had simply fallen in love with Hernán Cortés.

Some scholars have settled on another motive—revenge. They speculate that the woman may have held a grudge against the Aztecs for making her a slave. They even argue that La Malinche greatly exaggerated the amount of gold that Montezuma II kept in the Aztec capital of Tenochtitlan.[6]

Knowing how the Spaniards lusted after gold, La Malinche manipulated Cortés into marching to the capital to meet Montezuma II. Historians who believe revenge motivated La Malinche say the Spaniards were disappointed that upon meeting the Aztec ruler, he didn't have nearly as much gold as they thought he would.

raised his arms to speak. He told them that he was perfectly safe and urged them to return to their homes. He vouched once again for Cortés and told his people that the Spaniards meant them no harm. He told them Cortés and his entourage would soon be leaving.

There was a rumbling. Montezuma had seriously disappointed his people. They wondered how their ruler could continue to betray them. Suddenly, rocks and arrows besieged the balcony. Gravely wounded, Montezuma fell to the ground in agony. The sight of the fallen emperor led his subjects below to flee in terror.[7]

NEW SPAIN

No historical reports exist about Montezuma II's final days other than what the Spaniards documented. Their accounts say he refused to eat for the next few days and tore off the bandages when anyone tried to dress his wounds. Overcome with shame, the once great ruler evidently wanted to die.

Montezuma's Demise

By all accounts, Montezuma's condition worried Cortés. It's unclear if his concern was sincere or if Cortés feared how the Aztecs would react if their emperor died in Spanish custody. No one will ever know.

As Montezuma deteriorated, Cortés still had to deal with the angry Aztecs determined to storm his fortified quarters. He personally led a small raid of men on horses to try to disperse the crowd of Aztecs. He also set fire to their temples and ordered their statues destroyed before heading back to the palace.

Sure that the Aztecs would be ready to make peace, Cortés then asked La Malinche to translate for him. With their imprisoned emperor on his deathbed and their city in near ruins, the Aztecs had few options. But in this instance, La Malinche could not win the people over. Her words and charisma fell flat.

"You must now be convinced," she told the Aztec chiefs below, "that you have nothing further to hope from opposition

Charles Ricketts's beautiful painting shows the moment Montezuma II was mortally injured after urging the Aztecs to make peace with the Spanish invaders.

to the Spaniards. You have seen your gods trampled in the dust, your altars broken, your buildings burned, your warriors falling on all sides."[1]

She went on to say that there could still be peace if they put down their weapons and surrendered. But the Aztecs were unmoved by her words and no longer afraid. They vowed to fight to the end and were certain their gods would lead them to victory. This led Cortés to make plans to escape. The Aztecs greatly outnumbered his battle-weary and wounded men. To survive, the Spaniards would somehow have to leave unnoticed.

Meanwhile, Montezuma II's wounds continued taking their toll on his body. The last emperor of the Aztec Empire lay dying. In the early 1900s, historian Margaret Duncan Coxhead wrote an account of Montezuma II's final moments. She said that the Spaniards gave Montezuma II one more chance to convert to Christianity, but he would not abandon the faith of his fathers. Montezuma especially revered Huitzilopochtli, the Aztec god of war and the sun. Moreover, the Aztecs feared Quetzalcóatl, a god with a white beard they expected to return to rule their vast empire. Cortés's beard made Montezuma even more fearful of the Spaniard. Could he be Quetzalcóatl?

Before he died, Montezuma II supposedly put his children in Cortés's care and summoned La Malinche to interpret his last words. He reportedly begged her to ask the Spanish monarchy to look after the Mexican people as payment for the hospitality he showed Cortés and his companions.

"Your lord will do this," he purportedly said, "if it were only for the friendly offices I have rendered the Spaniards, and for the love I have shown them—though it has brought me to this condition. But for this I bear them no ill-will."[2]

Coxhead's account of these events, which drew heavily on Díaz del Castillo's recollections, seems very self-serving. The incidents that led to Montezuma's death had left him bitter, angry, and disgraced. Either he exercised extreme benevolence at the end of his life or this account is fiction.

In his retelling of what happened, Díaz del Castillo wrote a very touching account of the great leader's final moments while characterizing the Spaniards as loving and sympathetic. He wrote:

> "Cortés and all of us captains and soldiers wept for him, and there was no one among us that knew him and had dealings with him who did not mourn him as if he were our father, which was not surprising, since he was so good. It was stated that he had reigned for seventeen years, and was the best king they ever had in Mexico, and that he had personally triumphed in three wars against countries he had subjugated. I have spoken of the sorrow we all felt when we saw that Montezuma II was dead."[3]

How Montezuma II actually died and who killed him remains up for debate. But nearly everyone agrees that Cortés's arrival led to his demise. From there, the facts are few and far between.

Night Before the Dawn

After Montezuma II died, Cortés and his men tried to flee the city during the night, but the Aztecs attacked them from all sides. The battle, which took place June 30, 1520, amounted to a costly defeat for Cortés. It is now known as La Noche Triste, or "The Night of Sorrows." The number of casualties varies wildly from one account to the next, but it is clear that a significant number of Spaniards and their Tlaxcalan allies died in the battle. It's likely that more than a hundred Spaniards were killed and more than a thousand Tlaxcalans. Some of Montezuma II's children died during the battle as well. Cortés was escorting them out of the city.

After their demise, the bodies of Montezuma II and one of his chiefs were thrown into a canal. Exactly how Montezuma died remains unclear. Did his own people wound him or did the Spanish?

Who Really Killed Montezuma II?

Most accounts of Montezuma II's death are the same. They say that the Aztecs themselves, disillusioned with their powerless leader, pelted him with stones and arrows, causing a mortal injury.

But, of course, the only documented accounts of his death come from the Spaniards. Historians have tried to piece together bits and pieces of the Aztec version of events. These accounts suggest that the Spaniards killed the emperor after realizing he could no longer be of use to them.[4] In 2009, a British museum that showcased the life of Montezuma II offered the same version of how the emperor fell: the Aztecs didn't kill him; the Spaniards did.

The museum's curators pointed to two sixteenth-century manuscripts with illustrations that retell the events. The small figures in the drawings show Montezuma II shackled with a rope around his neck.[5] Does this prove the Spaniards murdered Montezuma II? We'll never know for certain.

Also lost during the night was the massive amount of gold Cortés and his men had plundered from the city. Somehow, a wounded Cortés and his weary party safely returned to Tlaxcala. There, they recovered from their injuries and plotted a final assault on the Aztec Empire. After numerous battles, the Aztecs finally surrendered on August 13, 1521. The once powerful Aztec Empire had crumbled.

Shortly after the empire's fall, La Malinche gave birth to a son, Martín, fathered by Cortés. Although the conquistador already had a wife in Spain, he gave Martín his last name, legitimizing him. European men during this time rarely gave children born out of wedlock their names. It's even more surprising that Cortés chose to do so for La Malinche's child. As an enslaved indigenous woman, European society did not view her as the conquistador's equal. Cortés also gave La Malinche tracts of land and a house. In New Spain, as Mexico was known, the Spanish denied landownership to anyone who didn't belong to their nobility[6]—making Cortés's gifts to La Malinche even more exceptional.

Cortés's actions reveal that he felt some affection for La Malinche. After all, she'd helped him take down an empire. But rather than taking her as his own, Cortés married her off to one of his soldiers, Don Juan Jaramillo, a nobleman. Cortés may have done this to prevent anyone from looking down on La Malinche as an unwed, indigenous mother.

Soon enough, Cortés became governor of New Spain. He'd finally landed a powerful position. But it would not last long. Due to lingering disputes between Cortés and the various people he'd alienated, the Spanish Crown eventually removed him from the post. Before his ouster, however, Cortés and his men traveled to what is now Honduras to quell a rebellion in 1524.

Naturally, he traveled with his trusted companion and interpreter La Malinche. This suggests that she may have been able to communicate, in yet another dialect, with the tribes of that region. If historical accounts of the trip are accurate, the Honduras expedition was nothing short of amazing.

During a stop in the province of Coatzacoalcos, Cortés ordered the noblemen there to gather in an open field so he could tell them about Christianity. There, Malinche encountered a pair of faces she recognized from years earlier. She spotted her mother, who sold her into slavery, and her half-brother, who was rewarded her inheritance.

When Cortés realized what was happening, he ordered La Malinche's family to come speak with her. The pair feared they

Cortés as Governor

After the Aztec Empire fell, King Charles of Spain appointed Hernán Cortés governor, captain general, and chief justice of this newly conquered territory. The Spanish named Mexico "New Spain of the Ocean Sea." Power hungry Cortés felt extremely disappointed when King Charles also appointed four others to help him govern the land.

Cortés viewed the king's move as an insult since his four assistants were to closely observe him and report back to the king. He felt that he had conquered the Aztecs on his own and wanted to rule their land on his own as well.

As governor, Cortés ordered the Aztec temples destroyed and began building what is now Mexico City. Because he'd made many enemies over the years, many people did not want Cortés to rule. He was constantly at odds with the Spanish Crown as a result. And while in Honduras in 1524, the monarchy removed him from power and summoned him back to Spain to answer for his behavior.

would be killed for what they had done. Instead, La Malinche forgave them. She told her mother and brother that she was happy, a Christian, and wife of a Spanish soldier. She might have been sold into slavery as a girl, but La Malinche had managed to overcome her circumstances.

She might have meant what she told her mother and brother. But she might have also just repeated the words Cortés had fed to her as part of his sermon. Díaz del Castillo captured the scene. He recalled, "(She said) that she would rather serve her husband and Cortés than anything else in the world, and would not exchange her place to be (ruler) of all the provinces in New Spain."[7]

LEGACY AND SHIFTING OPINIONS

Historians know very little about La Malinche after the Honduras expedition. After helping to "spawn a new race literally and symbolically,"[1] she basically vanished from public record. According to some accounts, she had a daughter with Jaramillo and lived out her years content to be a wife and mother. But others say she lived just a few more years after reuniting with her mother and half-brother. Additional reports say that she died in 1527 or 1528 after contracting smallpox during an epidemic.[2] If true, she would have been about twenty-five years old.

However, historian Sir Hugh Thomas believes she lived until at least 1550. He arrived at this theory by reviewing correspondence between New Spain residents and their contacts in Spain. When she did die, Cortés's family would have most likely raised Martín, while Jaramillo would have raised her daughter.

La Malinche's Legacy

La Malinche's legacy is a complicated one. As such, it has changed over time. Spain and the Catholic Church have

Hugh Thomas, an English historian specializing in Spanish history, is regarded as one of the most important experts on the Mexican conquest.

heralded her as a hero, since she helped to bring about Mexico's conquest and expedited the fall of the Aztec Empire. As the Spanish had deadlier weapons than the Aztecs, they likely would have conquered the territory without La Malinche's help. But their conquest would have required a lot more cannons, horses, gunpowder, and soldiers lost in battle. In short, they wouldn't have been able to conquer the land with so few losses without her assistance.

Although she helped the Spanish occupy Mexico, many indigenous people revered La Malinche at the time. For instance, the Tlaxcalans—allies of Cortés and enemies of the Aztecs—

considered her to be very special. In artwork that has survived from that time period, the Tlaxcalans often depict La Malinche as larger than Cortés as well as more colorful and animated. They show her negotiating with chiefs and rulers and with a shield riding into battle, while Cortés watches from a distance.[3]

She may have sided with the Spaniards over the Aztecs, but the Aztecs also viewed her as honorable. They and other indigenous groups referred to her as Malintzin, which denotes honor and respect. The Mexicans even named a volcano and various geographical sites after her.[4]

This engraving is based on the sixteenth-century codex "History of Tlaxcala." Notice how prominent La Malinche appears. It highlights her important role in the Mexican conquest.

La Llorona

Latin American folklore includes a ghost woman who constantly wails and grieves her loss. Her name is La Llorona, or the Crying Woman.

According to legend, La Llorona drowned her children in the river and then drowned herself after seeing what she had done. Now, she wanders the riverbanks in search of them. She causes misfortune and even death to those who get too close.

In one of the many incarnations of the legend, the weeping woman is none other than La Malinche, who felt jilted that Hernán Cortés left her for his noble Spanish wife. In this version of the legend, La Malinche killed their son and then herself.

Driven by her Aztec roots and Mexican pride, she took vengeance against the Spaniards as a ghost. Of course, we know that La Malinche did not kill her son with Cortés and seemed to live a happy, if short, life with her husband Juan Jaramillo.

The legend of the terrifying La Llorona is often told to children in Latin American countries as well as in the United States. Some believe she is the spirit of La Malinche, seeking vengeance against the Spaniards she served. Others believe she is simply a mother grieving for her dead children.

A legend in her own time, La Malinche has been characterized negatively and positively.

As Mexico's indigenous peoples began to resent rule by faraway Spain, they no longer viewed Hernán Cortés and La Malinche favorably. After three centuries of Spanish colonial rule, La Malinche had gone from the woman who brought them Christianity and saved them from Montezuma II's oppressive rule to a character akin to the serpent in the Garden of Eden. The people needed a scapegoat, someone to blame, and she fit. She was routinely portrayed as an indigenous woman whose lust for the white man led her to betray an entire nation. People even referred to her as the "whore of Cortés."[5]

As Mexican nationalism grew and the country struggled to free itself from Spanish rule during the 1800s and the Mexican Revolution of 1910, anti-Malinche sentiment hit its peak. While it's understandable that the people of a struggling nation would blame their woes on a young woman they think betrayed them, it doesn't make their conclusions about La Malinche accurate. After all, could she really have acted differently?

Remember that La Malinche was still a teenager when she became Cortés's interpreter. In contrast, the conquistador was already in his thirties, exuding confidence and an air of invincibility. He was intelligent, intense, and battle-tested. It's unrealistic to think that she could have outsmarted or betrayed Cortés, given their age gap and vastly different stations in life. She likely regarded Cortés as a sort of deity, as Montezuma II and many of the other native peoples did. Maybe she thought herself divinely chosen to help him in this great mission.[6] Also, remember that most of the tribes they encountered on their way to Montezuma II hated the Aztec leader. So, challenging Cortés would have also made La Malinche unpopular with these indigenous people.

Lastly, women of that time were expected to serve men. They were trained and taught to do so from the time they were little children. And since La Malinche was enslaved, she had even fewer rights than other women. She might have believed that to go against Cortés would have brought shame upon herself and her father's tribe.[7]

Today, public sentiment about La Malinche has changed again. Her story, her predicament, and her choices have come to symbolize the struggles that today's Chicanas face. "Chicana" (or "Chicano" for men and boys) means an American of Mexican descent. Alternately spelled Xicana or Xicano, the name comes from the Nahuatl word for the Mexica, an Aztec ethnic group. Award-winning Chicana author Sandra Cisneros is one of many to write about La Malinche in her work.

Much like many Chicanas today, La Malinche defied cultural expectations of what a woman's role should be. She freed herself from the chains of tradition[8], using her linguistic skills to elevate herself from slave status. She made herself more important to Cortés than many of the men in his forces.

Today, many women around the world still struggle with society's expectations for them. Sometimes, it is too dangerous for them to buck cultural norms. As La Malinche did, they may have to appease their oppressors just to survive. That being said, just what is Hernán Cortés's legacy?

Cortés's Legacy

Unlike the ever-shifting legacy that La Malinche leaves behind, Cortés remains an extremely controversial and unpopular person in Mexico. When Mexico won independence in 1810, a movement arose to separate the nation from its Spanish colonizers. Hence, Mexicans largely view Cortés as a brutal and cunning man who committed atrocities against the natives.

Chicana women today are finding their independence and breaking the mold of society's expectations. Some credit La Malinche for freeing herself from the "chains of tradition."

The Walking Dead?

Hernán Cortés's remains were moved several times after his death in 1547. He was initially buried in a Spanish mausoleum owned by the duke of Medina. But as more people died over the years, the duke's family needed the room and moved Cortés's body to a nearby church altar. But Cortés had asked to be buried in a Mexican monastery he'd commissioned to have built. Since the monastery was never completed, he was buried in New Spain near his mother and one of his sisters.

In 1629, Cortés's remains journeyed to a viceroy's palace and then to a Franciscan church in Mexico, where they stayed for eighty-seven years. After that, they moved to another room in the same church and from there the remains headed to a mausoleum and shrine at the Hospital of Jesus, which Cortés founded.

But concerns grew that his bones would be desecrated after Mexico won independence. So, the remains went to a secret location in the same hospital and were only rediscovered in 1946.

Finally, Mexican government bureau the Instituto Nacional de Antropología e Historia took custody of the remains.

Whew!

During the Cholulan massacre, for example, Cortés and his men slaughtered thousands of unarmed people to send a message to Montezuma II. The Spaniards also brought roughly thirty diseases to the Americas, killing millions of indigenous peoples as a result.

While Mexico views Cortés as a villain, some Europeans hold him in high regard for helping to spread Christianity to the Americas. They also laud him for achieving incredible

> *Hernán Cortés was moved eight times in the years after he died.*

victories in the face of seemingly insurmountable odds.

Ruthless and highly successful men like Cortés dominated the age of exploration. One could argue that if Cortés hadn't seized the opportunity to colonize the Americans, another European would have. But was Cortés more heartless than the typical conquistador? Was he also a cold-blooded murderer?

In 1522, after the Mexican conquest, Cortés's wife, Catalina, traveled from Spain to be with him. She knew her husband had a reputation for being a womanizer, and this likely unsettled Catalina. One night, after she and Cortés had an argument in public, the noblewoman died.

The authorities charged Cortés with her murder, but there was not enough evidence to find him guilty. After Catalina's murder, Jamaica governor Francisco de Garay met with Cortés in Mexico City. He wanted to acquire land. Three days later, however, Garay was found dead.[9] Cortés spent much of his later years defending himself against murder charges and accusations that he'd profiteered from the needless killings of Mexico's indigenous peoples.

In 1982, the president of Mexico commissioned a statue of Hernán Cortés, La Malinche, and their son, Martín. He wanted to place the statue near a site where Cortés once lived, but protests forced the government to move the monument. Today, it exists in relative obscurity in a little-known park. There, Cortés and La Malinche remain together, undisturbed by the outside world's opinions.

1485

Hernán Cortés is born in Medellín, Spain.

1499

Cortés's parents send him away to study Latin and law at University of Salamanca, but he fails and returns home.

1502

La Malinche is born to a noble Aztec family in a small Mexican village.

1504

Cortés sails to the Americas to make a name for himself and lands on the island of Hispaniola.

1511

Velázquez names Cortés one of Cuba's top officials. Hispaniola governor Diego Velázquez helps Cortés conquer Cuba.

1514

Cortés becomes a rancher in Cuba.

1518

Velázquez appoints Cortés captain of an expedition to Mexico but rescinds the order after they have a dispute.

1519

Cortés defies Velázquez and goes to Mexico, where he meets his interpreter La Malinche, now a slave.

1519

La Malinche and the other slave girls are baptized and given Christian names. Her new name is Marina, in honor of the Virgin Mary.

1519

Cortés takes over Veracruz.

1519

Cortés is named governor of "New Spain."

1520

Spanish forces suffer great losses in battle. Montezuma II dies.

1521

Aztec Empire falls.

1523

La Malinche gives birth to Cortés's son, Martín.

1528

Cortés returns to Spain facing murder charges.

1529

La Malinche may have died, but she also may have lived for decades afterward. Exactly when she died remains a mystery.

1530

Cleared of charges, Cortés returns to Mexico.

1536

Cortés goes on an expedition and finds Baja, California. He explores the region for a year before returning to Mexico.

1547

Cortés dies.

INTRODUCTION

1. "La Malinche—Translator and Companion to Cortés," Mexonline.com, http://www.mexonline.com/history-lamalinche.htm (accessed September 24, 2017).
2. Jean Franco, "La Malinche: from Gift to Sexual Contract," in *Critical Passions: Selected Essays* (Durham, NC: Duke University Press, 1999), pp. 66–79.

CHAPTER 1

Spanish Conquerors

1. Heather Whipps, "How the Spice Trade Changed the World." LiveScience.com, May 12, 2008, https://www.livescience.com/7495-spice-trade-changed-world.html.
2. Ibid.
3. William Gilbert, "Exploration and Discovery Beginnings of the Expansion of Europe," in *The Renaissance and Reformation* (Lawrence, KS: University of Kansas, 1998), http://vlib.iue.it/carrie/texts/carrie_books/gilbert.
4. Ibid.
5. Heather Pringle, "How Europeans Brought Sickness to the New World," *Science Magazine*, June 4, 2015, http://www.sciencemag.org/news/2015/06/how-europeans-brought-sickness-new-world Retrieved 9/24/17.
6. Ibid.
7. Ibid.

8. Nathan Nunn and Nancy Qian, "The Columbian Exchange: A History of Disease, Food and Ideas," *Journal of Economic Perspectives*, Spring 2010, https://www.aeaweb.org/articles?id=10.1257/jep.24.2.163.

9. Julia Calderone, "Christopher Columbus Brought a Host of Terrible New Diseases to the New World." *Business Insider*, Oct. 12, 2015, http://www.business insider.com/diseases-columbus-brought-to-americas-2015-10.

10. Ibid.

11. David J. Meltzer, "How Columbus Sickened the New World: Why Were Native Americans So Vulnerable to the Diseases European Settlers Brought with Them," *New Scientist*, Oct. 10, 1992, https://www.newscientist.com/article/mg13618424-700-how-columbus-sickened-the-new-world-why-were-native-americans-so-vulnerable-to-the-diseases-european-settlers-brought-with-them.

12. Nunn and Qian.

CHAPTER 2

Humble Beginnings

1. Nancy Stanley and Sirena Turner, "Hernán Cortés: The Man Behind the Mystique," *Chrestomathy: Annual Review of Undergraduate Research School of Humanities and Social Sciences College of Charleston*, Volume 3, 2003, http://chrestomathy.cofc.edu/documents/vol3/stanley-and-turner.pdf.

2. Ibid.

3. Ibid.

4. Leo Africanus, "The History and Description of Africa," The Hakluyt Society, London, 1600, https://archive.org/stream/historyanddescr03porygoog#page/n6/mode/2up.

5. Stanley and Turner.

6. Ibid.

7. The Mariners Museum, "Hernán Cortés," http://ageofex.marinersmuseum.org/index.php?type=explorer&id=34 (accessed October 1, 2017).

8. Hugh Thomas, *Conquest: Montezuma II, Cortés, and the Fall of Old Mexico*, (New York, NY: Simon and Schuster, 1993).

9. Ibid.

CHAPTER 3

The New World

1. Nancy Stanley and Sirena Turner, "Hernán Cortés: The Man Behind the Mystique," *Chrestomathy: Annual Review of Undergraduate Research School of Humanities and Social Sciences College of Charleston, Volume 3, 2003*, http://chrestomathy.cofc.edu/documents/vol3/stanley-and-turner.pdf.

2. Richard Lee Marks, *Cortés: The Great Adventurer and the Fate of Aztec Mexico*, (New York, NY: Alfred A. Knopf Publishers, 1993).

3. Stanley and Turner.

4. Francis Augustus MacNutt, "Fernándo Cortés: His Five Letters of Relation to the Emperor Charles V," 1908, https://archive.org/stream/fernandocorteshi01cort/fernandocorteshi01cort_djvu.txt.

5. Manuel Aguilar Moreno, *Handbook to Life in the Aztec World* (New York, NY: Oxford University Press, 2006), https://tinyurl.com/ya6xwxz5.
6. MacNutt.
7. Moreno.

CHAPTER 4

La Malinche

1. Ed Morawski, "Goddess of the Grass: The Story of Malinalli," https://malincheinfo.wordpress.com/the-girl (accessed October 5, 2017).
2. Cordelia Candelaria, "La Malinche, Feminist Prototype," Frontiers Editorial Collective, 1980, http://www.latinamericanstudies.org/aztecs/Malinche.pdf (accessed 10/5/17).
3. Ibid.
4. Bernal Díaz del Castillo, *The Memoirs of the Conquistador Bernal Díaz—A True and Full Account of the Discovery and Conquest of Mexico and New Spain*, The Hakluyt Society, 1632, https://archive.org/details/tesisnoqueprese00garcgoog.
5. Rosario Perez-Lagunes, *The Myth of La Malinche: From the Chronicles to Modern Mexican Theater* (Blacksburg, VA: Virginia Polytechnic University Press, 2001), http://citeseerx.ist.psu.edu/viewdoc/download?doi=10.1.1.500.5250&rep=rep1&type=pdf.
6. Ibid.
7. Patricia de Fuentes, ed. and trans., *The Conquistadors: First-Person Accounts of the Conquest of Mexico* (Norman, OK: University of Oklahoma Press, 1993) p. 138.

CHAPTER 5
Partnership

1. Bernal Díaz del Castillo, *The Memoirs of the Conquistador Bernal Díaz—A True and Full Account of the Discovery and Conquest of Mexico and New Spain*, The Hakluyt Society, 1632, https://archive.org/details/tesisnoqueprese00garcgoog, p. 128.
2. Castillo, p. 131.
3. Edwin Williamson, *The Penguin History of Latin America* (New York, NY: Penguin Books, 1992) p. 18.
4. Christopher Minster, "The Cholula Massacre," Thoughtco.com, September 8, 2017, https://www.thoughtco.com/the-cholula-massacre-2136527.
5. Ibid.
6. Ibid.

CHAPTER 6
La Malinche to the Rescue

1. Christopher Minster, "The Cholula Massacre," Thoughtco.com, September 8, 2017, https://www.thoughtco.com/the-cholula-massacre-2136527.
2. Bernal Díaz del Castillo, *The Memoirs of the Conquistador Bernal Díaz—A True and Full Account of the Discovery and Conquest of Mexico and New Spain*, The Hakluyt Society, 1632, https://archive.org/details/tesisnoqueprese00garcgoog.
3. Helen Ward Banks, *The Boys' Prescott* (New York, NY: Frederick Stokes Company, 1916).
4. Ibid.
5. Díaz del Castillo.
6. Banks.

CHAPTER 7

Cortés Meets Montezuma II

1. Helen Ward Banks, *The Boys' Prescott* (New York, NY: Frederick Stokes Company, 1916).
2. Mark Cartwright, "Tenochtitlan," Ancient History, September 25, 2013, https://www.ancient.eu/ Tenochtitlan.
3. Ibid.
4. Banks.
5. Ibid.
6. Ibid.
7. Bernal Díaz del Castillo, *The Memoirs of the Conquistador Bernal Díaz—A True and Full Account of the Discovery and Conquest of Mexico and New Spain*, The Hakluyt Society, 1632, https://archive.org/details/ tesisnoqueprese00garcgoog.
8. Ibid.
9. Ibid.
10. Ibid.
11. The History Channel, "Aztec Warriors: Weapons and Armor," https://www.historyonthenet.com/aztec-warriors-weapons-and-armor/ (accessed October 27, 2017).

CHAPTER 8

The Fall of the Aztec Empire

1. Bernal Díaz del Castillo, *The Memoirs of the Conquistador Bernal Díaz—A True and Full Account of the Discovery and Conquest of Mexico and New Spain*, The Hakluyt Society, 1632, https://archive.org/details/ tesisnoqueprese00garcgoog.

2. Ibid.
3. Helen Ward Banks, *The Boys' Prescott* (New York, NY: Frederick Stokes Company, 1916).
4. Ibid.
5. William H. Prescott, *History of the Conquest of Mexico* (New York, NY: Harper & Brothers, 1843).
6. Bob Schulman, "The Man Behind the Sword of Cortés," Huffington Post, March 25, 2014, https://www.huffingtonpost.com/bob-schulman/mexicos-la-malinche-the-w_b_4996509.html.
7. Banks.

CHAPTER 9

New Spain

1. Helen Ward Banks, *The Boys' Prescott* (New York, NY: Frederick Stokes Company, 1916).
2. Margaret Duncan Coxhead, *Romance of History: Mexico* (New York, NY: Frederick A. Stokes Company, 1909), http://www.mainlesson.com/display.php?author=kelly&book=mexico&story=_front.
3. Bernal Díaz del Castillo, *The Memoirs of the Conquistador Bernal Díaz—A True and Full Account of the Discovery and Conquest of Mexico and New Spain*, The Hakluyt Society, 1632, https://archive.org/details/tesisnoqueprese00garcgoog.
4. Arifa Akbar, "Aztec Ruler Unmasked," *Independent*, April 12, 2009, http://www.independent.co.uk/arts-entertainment/art/features/aztec-ruler-moctezuma-unmasked-1668030.html.
5. Ibid.
6. Cordelia Candelaria, "La Malinche, Feminist Prototype," Frontiers Editorial Collective, 1980,

http://www.latinamericanstudies.org/aztecs/
Malinche.pdf (accessed October 5, 2017).
7. Díaz del Castillo.

CHAPTER 10

Legacy and Shifting Opinions

1. Cordelia Candelaria, "La Malinche, Feminist
   Prototype," Frontiers Editorial Collective, 1980,
   http://www.latinamericanstudies.org/aztecs/
   Malinche.pdf (accessed October 5, 2017).
2. Ibid.
3. Julee Tate, "La Malinche: The Shifting Legacy of
   a Transcultural Icon," *Latin Americanist*, May 11
   2017, http://onlinelibrary.wiley.com/doi/10.1111/
   tla.12102/pdf.
4. Candelaria.
5. Tate
6. Candelaria
7. Ibid.
8. Tate.
9. Nancy Stanley and Sirena Turner, "Hernán Cortés:
   The Man Behind the Mystique," *Chrestomathy: Annual
   Review of Undergraduate Research School of Humanities
   and Social Sciences College of Charleston*, Volume 3, 2003,
   http://chrestomathy.cofc.edu/documents/vol3/
   stanley-and-turner.pdf.

allegiance Loyalty to a person, group, country, or cause.

ascension A rise to the top, especially to a powerful position.

ceremonial Describes a celebration having to do with a formal event.

decimate To destroy a large percentage of something.

demise A person's death or the end of something.

emissary A person sent on a very important mission.

indigenous Native to a particular country or region for generations.

inheritance Money, land, or property that is received when someone dies.

intriguing Interesting; sparking curiosity.

nationalism Feelings of patriotism and pride in your own country.

perplexing Baffling or hard to understand.

prominence Having importance in society.

shrewd Clever.

skirmish A minor fight or small battle away from a major battle.

treachery A betrayal of trust.

BOOKS

Anderson, Zachary. *Hernán Cortés: Conquering the Aztec Empire.* New York, NY: Cavendish Square Publishing, 2014.

Owens, Lisa L. *A Journey with Hernán Cortés.* Minneapolis, MN: Lerner Publications, 2017.

Serrano, Francisco, and Pablo Serrano. *La Malinche: The Princess Who Helped Cortés Conquer an Empire.* Toronto, Canada: Groundwood Books, 2012.

Siepel, Kevin H. *Conquistador Voices: The Spanish Conquest of the Americas as Recounted Largely by the Participants.* Angola, NY: Spruce Tree Press, 2015.

WEBSITES

Aztec History Online
http://www.aztec-history.com/fall-of-the-aztec-empire.html
A comprehensive and chronological look at the fall of an empire.

Online Guide to Mexico
http://www.mexonline.com/history-lamalinche.htm
An easy-to-read history of Mexico's conquest.

FILMS

Conquistadors (2001, PBS)